CAULIFLOWER POWER

CAULIFLOWER POWER

75 Feel-Good, Gluten-Free Recipes
Made with the World's Most Versatile Vegetable

LINDSAY GRIMES
FREEDMAN

Photographs by Lauren Volo

Artisan | New York

···

Library of Congress Cataloging-in-Publication Data

Names: Freedman, Lindsay Grimes, author.
Title: Cauliflower power / by Lindsay Grimes Freedman
Description: New York, NY : Artisan, a division of
    Workman Publishing Co., Inc., [2020]
Includes index.
Identifiers: LCCN 2019018632 | ISBN 9781579659011
    (hardcover : alk. paper)
Subjects: LCSH: Cooking (Vegetables) | LCGFT:
Cookbooks.
Classification: LCCTX801 .F654 2020 | DDC641.6/5—dc23
LC record available on https://lccn.com.gov/2019018632

···

Design by Headcase Design

Artisan books are available at special discounts when purchased in bulk for premiums and sales promotions as well as for fund-raising or educational use. Special editions or book excerpts also can be created to specification. For details, contact the Special Sales Director at the address below, or send an e-mail to specialmarkets@workman.com.

Contact speakersbureau@workman.com for speaking engagements.

Published by Artisan
A division of Workman Publishing Co., Inc.
225 Varick Street
New York, NY 10014-4381
artisanbooks.com

Artisan is a registered trademark of Workman Publishing Co., Inc.

Published simultaneously in Canada by Thomas Allen & Son, Limited

Printed in China

First printing, December 2019

10 9 8 7 6 5 4 3 2 1

To my husband, Jaryd, for your love, your jokes, and your late-night grocery runs to buy cauliflower. I couldn't do this without you.

To our boys, Caleb and Nolan. You are what makes life good.
This is for you.

CONTENTS

1

BREAKFAST **20**

3

HAPPY HOUR **100**

5

SIDES **168**

2

LUNCH 76

4

DINNER 124

6

DESSERTS 206

INTRODUCTION

EVEN THE MOST casual cook has likely noticed the recent transformation of cauliflower. No longer the drab, steamed punishment on your childhood dinner plate, cauliflower is now the "it" vegetable, beloved by vegans, vegetarians, and omnivores alike. Whether you find your local restaurant offering a cauliflower-crust pizza or boxes of cauliflower pasta lining grocery store shelves, it's easy to see that cauliflower is having a moment. Well, not just a moment, but rather an evolution of culinary creativity leading to a golden age for this versatile vegetable.

Some people might roll their eyes at the thought of an entire book of recipes based on cauliflower. I get it. For decades, cauliflower was a bland, raw floret relegated to the most ignored spot on a crudité platter, always the last to go. To those cauliflower skeptics, those living in the past of what cauliflower once was, I challenge you to adjust your vegetable paradigm. Cauliflower is a chameleon—with a few easy-to-master techniques, it can morph from a sturdy brassica into a creamy sauce, a crunchy granola, or even the perfect base for bread or fudgy brownies. Its ability to adapt and embrace flavors makes cauliflower the perfect vehicle for almost any taste, from sweet to savory.

I've been closely following the resurgence of this once-slandered veg since starting my food blog in 2014. But my first run-in with cauliflower that was far from the classic floret occurred in college, before Instagram and, well, even before I began cooking for myself (beyond the occasional microwaved ramen). It was around 2007, and that holiday season there was a buzz about cauliflower mash. This new, healthful alternative to the classic potato side dish was showing up in lifestyle magazines and on websites. Though many of us were skeptical at the time, once we tried the light and creamy mash we began to understand and appreciate cauliflower's ability to stand in for indulgent white potatoes.

Once cauliflower mash became common, the vegetable was reinvented once again. Cauliflower pizza crust first made its appearance in 2009, when a blogger wrote about her experiments in substituting cauliflower rice for all-purpose flour in a traditional pizza crust recipe. It turned out so well that this creativity quickly inspired home cooks everywhere to try their own spins on the idea.

Why did people take notice? The health benefits of eating cauliflower couldn't be ignored. Part of cauliflower's rise stems from its versatility and ability to fit into a wide variety of diets and lifestyles. Whether your diet is low carb, keto, gluten-free, paleo, Whole30, or vegan, cauliflower is a tasty addition to your ingredient lineup. Its ability to transcend dietary lines is part of the reason cauliflower has made its way into many people's kitchens.

In addition, cauliflower is loaded with nutritional and health benefits. It is a powerhouse of vitamin C, fiber, and antioxidants. The nutrients in cauliflower help reduce the risk of cancer, heart disease, and brain disorders; fight inflammation; improve digestion; and aid in weight loss. Another reason for cauliflower's popularity is its ability to take on many forms. It can morph seamlessly from a whole head to dehydrated crumbs to a creamy sauce. Parents desperate to work more vegetables into their kids' meals have found cauliflower to be the perfect partner.

The cauliflower pizza crust trend prompted chefs and home cooks alike to start thinking outside the floret and to experiment with the cauliflower in all its different forms. Cauliflower now has a prominent place on restaurant menus all over the country. Whether as a side dish or a main course, cauliflower is no longer an afterthought but the star of the meal.

ABOUT ME

Cauliflower became a staple in my kitchen in 2011 when my husband was diagnosed with type 1 diabetes. Lamenting the days of carefree eating, I began looking for low-glycemic alternatives for some of his favorite foods. One of my first forays into low-carb cooking was perfecting a cauliflower pizza crust of my own, so we could once again indulge in our favorite food together.

Overall, though, I found it difficult to find recipes that incorporated the flavors and ingredients we loved and that also fit within our new dietary needs. These frustrations led me to experiment and to create recipes we could both savor and enjoy. After years of finding my way in the kitchen, I launched my food blog, *The Toasted Pine Nut*, to share my creations in hopes of helping others in a similar situation.

Over the past several years, both my blog and our family have grown. We now have two perfectly crazy boys in the mix, which has forced me to become more creative in the kitchen to satisfy their picky palates. Because of its versatility, cauliflower has become a cornerstone in most of our meals.

HOW TO MAKE THE MOST OF THIS BOOK

I've written this book as a compendium of cauliflower recipes for the home cook. From breakfast to dinner, from rice to steaks, from sweet to savory, I hope to inspire home cooks to experiment with cauliflower and see all that it can add to your meals. Use these recipes as a starting point and then maybe dream up something new.

When you dive into the seventy-five-plus different recipes featuring your new favorite superfood, you'll find dishes for everything from breakfast (smoothies, muffins, and cauliflower granola) and lunch (kale Caesar salad, rainbow rolls, and cauliflower falafel) through dinner (cauliflower-based gnocchi and the most mouthwatering veggie burgers you've ever had) and dessert (brownies, chewy white chocolate cookies, and cauliflower rice pudding), plus side dishes (mac and cheese, Cheddar-jalapeño biscuits, and spicy churros) and even happy hour treats (skillet nachos, cauliflower hummus, and buffalo cauliflower wings that cannot be missed).

Many of the recipes are vegan and vegetarian, although there are some made with cheese and butter, and even a few that include lean fish, chicken, or beef to round out all the vegetable goodness. These recipes can be customized to fit your own dietary needs and lifestyle. If a recipe calls for butter or cheese, feel free to swap in your favorite nondairy brand. If you're not a big meat eater, try my favorite vegetarian alternatives—sautéed tempeh or tofu.

When you head to the grocery store or farmer's market, look for a cauliflower head without any brown spots. Cauliflower comes in a few different colors—just make sure the top outer florets are not sporting any brown spots (this could indicate the head is almost past its prime). A few leaves are typically still attached.

Also keep in mind the amount of cauliflower required for the recipe. If the recipe calls for 1 to 2 cups, search for a smaller head so you don't have a lot of leftover florets (and if you do, see page 16 for how to use them). A recipe that uses 4 or more cups will require a head on the larger size. Cauliflower is pretty hardy, so it will keep in your fridge for about a week. I store it unwrapped in the vegetable drawer, but wrapping it in plastic wrap or putting it in an airtight bag or container may keep it fresh even longer.

Catching on to the cauliflower trend, grocery stores now offer precut cauliflower in various forms, from fresh or frozen florets to fresh or frozen cauliflower rice. Precut cauliflower can be a great time-saver, but just make sure you further cut or prep the cauliflower in the same form and size called for in the recipe, because prepackaged florets and rice aren't always consistently sized.

Before you start cooking, turn to page 13 to learn the five main ways to prep cauliflower: the whole head, steaks, florets, rice, and meal. These methods will be used throughout the recipes in this book and you can refer to them as needed.

My goal in creating these recipes was to keep them as approachable as possible, so only a few tools are required, and they're ones you likely already have in your kitchen. The two tools consistently used are a high-powered blender and a food processor. A high-powered blender is used to break down cauliflower for sauces, dressings, and batters. It can cream the cauliflower into a smooth and even consistency. A food processor is essential not only to prep the cauliflower when making rice or meal, but also to transform cauliflower into doughs and spreads. If you only own a food processor or maybe even just a handheld immersion blender, you can still create most of the recipes in the book. Just keep in mind the consistency the recipe calls for and blend or process the mixture until that consistency is achieved.

And if you don't have a food processor, you can still make cauliflower rice. Use the largest holes of a handheld box grater to transform cauliflower into rice. This process takes a bit longer and needs more muscle power, but works just as well.

Since it's always a draw to dirty as few prep bowls as possible, many of these recipes are made completely in the food processor or blender, which makes for faster and easier cleanup. Where applicable, I also give some ideas on how to store leftovers. (Although, in my experience with these recipes, leftovers were nonexistent.)

Once you start cooking with cauliflower you'll find endless ways to incorporate it into your diet. Cauliflower rice, mash, and pizza crust are so widespread that we can now feel confident using cauliflower in our breakfast parfait, salad dressings, pasta dough, and even cookie batter. Oprah gave cauliflower her stamp of approval and recently came out with her own line of cauliflower pizza crust, and a certain familiar blue box now offers a cauliflower-infused mac-and-cheese line. While the convenience of the new flurry of cauliflower products is tempting, nothing compares to a homemade cauliflower masterpiece that you make for your friends and family all by yourself.

THE FIVE KEY WAYS TO PREPARE CAULIFLOWER

AS YOU COOK through this book, you'll notice that the five key ways to prepare cauliflower are used over and over. So instead of repeating the instructions in each recipe, I created this step-by-step tutorial. Start here to learn everything you need to know to prep cauliflower. You'll get both in-depth instructions and a visual cue for each technique.

To work with cauliflower, you should have a sharp knife and a stable cutting board, a food processor with a grating/shredding attachment as well as the main chopping blade, and cheesecloth or a clean, thin dish towel. In many of the recipes, like the dressings and batters where you need to break the cauliflower down completely, a high-powered blender is also useful.

When you read a recipe, you'll notice it calls for a certain amount of cauliflower already prepped a certain way, such as florets or rice. Refer back to this section as needed.

After making a few recipes, you'll get the hang of it. However, when a recipe requires cauliflower meal, I've chosen to list florets and take you through the process of making the meal in each individual recipe. The reason for this is that some meal is cooked before you squeeze out the excess moisture, and some is squeezed raw. Regardless, I think it's important to give you a visual of what the meal should look like when you're finished and the process it takes to get there, so I've included the method here as well.

WHOLE HEAD

This is the easiest way to prepare cauliflower because it requires only basic knife skills. When picking out a whole cauliflower, go for aesthetics. Look for one that is round, with no brown spots, and would look good sitting as a centerpiece on your table (not that you're going to use it that way!).

Wash and dry the cauliflower head. Use your hands to peel back and break off the leaves. If there are any stubborn leaves or ones that didn't break off cleanly, use a small paring knife to slice away any remaining green leaf stumps. If there is a longer, protruding stem, slice it off with a sharp knife so that the cauliflower sits flat on your counter. Don't cut into the floret branches. Instead, keep the entire head intact.

A whole head of cauliflower is best steamed or roasted, and then served with a really delicious spice rub or sauce.

STEAKS

When you want to turn a whole cauliflower into steaks, buy a larger head that can produce several good-size slabs. Depending on the number of people you're feeding, you might need to buy more than one head to ensure you have enough of the same size steaks. It's important to note that what keeps a steak intact is the center stem of the cauliflower. So, it's not important how big and round the cauliflower is, but rather how wide the stem is—something you can never really tell until you cut into it.

Wash and dry the cauliflower head. Remove and discard the outer leaves. Cut off any protruding stem so that the cauliflower sits flat on the cutting board. Use a long, sharp knife to cut the head in half from the top down. Hold one half of the cauliflower and cut ½-inch (1 cm) slices away from the center. Repeat with the second half. Each head will make 2 to 4 steaks, depending on the size of the stem. Save any florets that fall from the head for use in another recipe.

Steaks can be seasoned and grilled, roasted in the oven, or cooked on the stovetop.

FLORETS

Florets may be the most traditional way of eating cauliflower. Any size head can easily be turned into florets.

First, wash and dry the cauliflower. Remove and discard the outer leaves. Turn the head upside down on a cutting board and use a sharp knife to cut the florets away from the center stem (which you can discard). Cut the florets into medium or smaller florets (as directed in the recipe) and discard any long unwanted stems.

One small head of cauliflower weighs about 22 ounces (640 grams) and yields 3 cups (400 grams) of florets. A medium head

weighs about 34 ounces (960 grams) and yields 4 to 5 cups (530 to 665 grams) of florets. A larger head of cauliflower can weigh 45 ounces (1.3 kg) or more and can make 6 cups (800 grams) or more of florets.

Many grocery stores now sell precut florets, which is a great time-saver. Just make sure you cut them down to the uniform size called for in the recipe.

Florets can be eaten raw with dip, roasted, or cooked on the stovetop. They're also great fried and served with a dipping sauce, such as Green Goddess Dressing (page 200).

RICE

To make cauliflower rice, you'll need a food processor fitted with the shredding attachment.

Prepare cauliflower florets (see page 16). Then drop the florets into the feed tube of the food processor and, with the machine running, press them through the shredder with the pusher insert. If you are prepping more than one head of cauliflower, you may need to work in batches and transfer the rice from the bottom compartment to a large bowl.

If you don't have a food processor, you can shred a cauliflower head through the biggest holes of a handheld grater.

One small head of cauliflower makes about 3 cups (315 grams) of cauliflower rice.

A medium head makes 4 to 5 cups (420 to 525 grams) and a large head makes about 6 cups (630 grams) of rice.

Cauliflower rice, if eaten by itself, is best pan-fried and dressed up with different spices (see page 170). It can also be blended with other ingredients and transformed into delicious sauces and baked goods.

Grocery stores now sell cauliflower rice and cauliflower "pearls," which are usually cut-up cauliflower stems. These options can be great time-savers, but make sure the rice or pearls are uniform and your desired size. Shredding cauliflower rice at home, although a bit messy, gives me the long rice shape that I love.

MEAL

Prepare cauliflower florets (see page 16). Working in batches and using the chopping blade, process 1 cup of florets for about 20 seconds, until the florets are completely chopped into a meal, a bit finer than rice. The meal should have a grainy, moist consistency with pieces a bit bigger than you'd find in a nut flour.

Transfer the meal to a bowl and repeat until all the florets are processed. Some recipes will say to immediately place the meal on a clean, thin dish towel or piece of cheesecloth and squeeze out the liquid (The more liquid you can squeeze, the better the recipe will be!). Other recipes require you to cook or warm the meal first before squeezing out the excess moisture.

One head of cauliflower makes about ½ cup (57 grams) to 1 cup (113 grams) of meal after the excess liquid has been squeezed out. Cauliflower meal is best used in batters and then baked into a pizza crust (page 143) or Cheddar-Jalapeño Cauliflower Biscuits (page 205).

1

BREAKFAST

TRADITIONAL BREAKFAST FOODS tend not to be the healthiest of our day. In common breakfast meals, ranging from loaded eggs served with bacon to starchy breads, pancake stacks, and sugar-infused cereal, vegetables are hard to come by. Now, I'm not one to turn down any of the aforementioned breakfast foods, really, but I also love the concept of using the most versatile vegetable to insert some nutrients and unexpected pizzazz into a meal that is typically lacking in both. Whether you're making a classic waffle, cinnamon chocolate scones, or a savory skillet of eggs and hash, cauliflower can be a truly nutritious and versatile addition to your morning meal.

.... ✳ ....

DOUBLE-CHOCOLATE GRANOLA PARFAIT CUPS

....

DOUBLE-CHOCOLATE OAT-FREE GRANOLA may sound decadent, but it's a nutrient-dense way to start your day. Hemp hearts are a slightly nutty-tasting, plant-based protein that is easy to incorporate into your daily routine. The protein punch is nicely balanced with the flax seeds, which give you a good dose of fiber and omega-3 fatty acids.

**MAKES 3 CUPS;
SERVES 4 TO 6**

....

FOR THE GRANOLA

- 1½ cups (182 g) chopped raw pecans
- 1 cup (175 g) chopped raw hazelnuts
- ¼ cup (21 g) unsweetened shredded coconut
- ¼ cup (40 g) hemp hearts
- ¼ cup (40 g) flax seeds
- ¼ cup (40 g) coconut sugar
- ¼ cup (24 g) cocoa powder
- 1½ cups (158 g) cauliflower rice (see page 18)
- ¼ cup (60 g) ghee (see Note)
- ¼ cup (64 g) natural peanut butter (see Note)
- ¼ cup (83 g) agave nectar (see Note)
- ½ cup (87 g) 60% cacao dark chocolate chips

(continued)

1. Position racks in the middle and top of the oven. Preheat the oven to 350°F (180°C). Line a baking sheet with parchment paper.

2. In a large bowl, combine the pecans, hazelnuts, coconut, hemp hearts, flax seeds, coconut sugar, and cocoa powder. Add the cauliflower rice and stir until well combined.

3. In a medium saucepan over medium heat, whisk together the ghee, peanut butter, and agave nectar. Once the sauce is well mixed and has thickened a bit, about 2 minutes, remove from the heat.

4. Pour the peanut sauce over the nut and seed mixture and fold in the sauce until everything is completely coated.

5. Spread the wet granola mixture in a single layer on the prepared baking sheet. Don't worry if it's a bit clumpy; the clumps will end up becoming delicious clusters.

6. Bake for 15 minutes, then use a spatula to gently stir the granola. Bake for another 7 minutes, or until the granola feels dry.

CONTINUED ·················

FOR THE PARFAIT

- 3 cups (735 g) whole-milk yogurt
- Banana slices (optional)
- Fresh berries (optional)
- 3 tablespoons natural peanut butter (optional)

7. Move the baking sheet to the top rack and turn off the oven, keeping the door shut. Allow the granola to dry out and cool completely for about 30 minutes. Once it has cooled to room temperature, remove the granola from the oven and stir in the chocolate chips.

8. Assemble the parfaits: Layer the granola and yogurt in a parfait glass or cup. Top with your choice of bananas, fresh berries, or a dab of peanut butter. The granola will keep for up to 1 week stored in an airtight container in the fridge.

Note: You can substitute ingredients based on what you have on hand or what you prefer. Peanut butter can be replaced with almond butter or another nut butter, you can use Greek yogurt or nondairy yogurt instead of whole-milk yogurt, and agave nectar can easily be replaced with honey or maple syrup. Ghee is clarified butter, but you can use regular butter or coconut oil.

Note: Both agave nectar and coconut nectar are low-glycemic sweeteners that you can use in place of traditional sugar. If you aren't concerned with the glycemic index, honey or maple syrup works just as well.

PEANUT BUTTER AND BERRY SMOOTHIE

MY KIDS LOVE to hijack—I mean share—my smoothies. As long as the drink is pretty and colorful, I can usually sneak some veggies into it without them noticing. This recipe requires you to prep the cauliflower the night before you blend the smoothie. Every weekend, I like to steam an entire head of riced cauliflower and freeze it so I can easily add ½ cup (53 g) at a time to smoothies throughout the week. Have some leftover smoothie? Pour into popsicle molds and freeze for an afterschool snack.

MAKES ABOUT 4 SMOOTHIES

- ½ cup (53 g) cauliflower rice (see page 18)
- 2 cups (288 g) frozen mixed berries
- 1 cup (240 mL) unsweetened vanilla almond milk
- ½ banana, frozen (see Note)
- 2 tablespoons natural peanut butter
- 2 tablespoons agave nectar, honey, or maple syrup (see Note, page 25)

1. Bring an inch of water to a boil in a small saucepan. Place the cauliflower rice in a steamer basket set over the boiling water. Cover and steam the rice for 3 to 5 minutes, until the edges of the rice appear translucent. Since you're prepping this ahead, think about ricing, steaming, and freezing an entire head of cauliflower for easy weekday morning smoothies.

2. Transfer the rice to a bag or container and freeze overnight or for at least 3 hours. The cauliflower will keep for about 3 months in the freezer.

3. The next morning, place ½ cup (53 g) frozen cauliflower rice, the berries, almond milk, banana, peanut butter, and agave nectar in a high-powered blender. Blend on high for 1 minute, until completely smooth. (Depending on your blender, you may need to take breaks to scrape down the sides with a rubber spatula and push the frozen food around to get things moving.)

4. The smoothies are best when served immediately.

Note: Using frozen bananas and cauliflower makes for a really thick smoothie that is almost the consistency of soft-serve ice cream and can be eaten with a spoon. As soon as you have bananas that start to get spotty, slice them into pieces and throw them in a large bag in the freezer so you always have some ready for smoothies.

CHOCOLATE HAZELNUT CHIA PUDDING

WAKING UP TO a jar of premade chocolate chia pudding in your fridge makes for not only a seamless morning, but also an indulgent and healthful way to start your day. Chia pudding is similar in consistency to a tapioca pudding; the hazelnuts and cauliflower rice add a hearty and satisfying crunch.

SERVES 2

- 1 13.5-ounce (398 mL) can unsweetened coconut cream (preferably Thai Kitchen or Native Forest brand)
- 1 teaspoon refined coconut oil
- 1 cup (105 g) cauliflower rice (see page 18)
- ¼ teaspoon sea salt
- ½ cup (96 g) chia seeds
- ½ cup (57 g) chopped raw hazelnuts, plus more for topping
- 3 tablespoons agave nectar, coconut nectar, honey, or maple syrup (see Note, page 25)
- 2 tablespoons cocoa powder
- 1 teaspoon vanilla bean powder
- 4 tablespoons dark chocolate chips (optional), for topping

1. Pour the coconut cream into a large Mason jar (or any jar with a lid that's large enough to hold all the ingredients). If the coconut cream is clumpy, microwave it for 30 seconds to 1 minute, then secure the lid and shake. This will get rid of the clumps and ensure that the cream is smooth. Alternatively, you can warm it on the stovetop in a saucepan over medium-high heat, whisking it constantly for about 3 minutes until smooth before pouring it into the jar.

2. Heat the coconut oil in a small skillet over medium-high heat. Add the cauliflower rice and salt and cook for about 5 minutes, stirring frequently. The cauliflower rice should not brown, but just cook through. Reduce the heat if it starts to brown. Add the cauliflower rice to the jar and let cool.

3. Add the chia seeds, hazelnuts, agave nectar, cocoa powder, and vanilla bean powder to the jar.

4. Screw on the lid and shake vigorously to combine. Keep this chia pudding in a large jar in the fridge if you plan on spooning it out into bowls in the morning. But if you are prepping single-serve breakfasts, divide the pudding between two smaller jars and top with chopped hazelnuts and chocolate chips.

5. Refrigerate for at least 2 hours or overnight. The pudding will keep for about 10 days in the refrigerator.

TRAIL MIX BREAKFAST COOKIES

YES, YOU CAN eat cookies for breakfast—especially when they're filled with cauliflower and protein-packed nuts and seeds. You can customize the cookies by swapping in different nuts, seeds, and dried fruit. They're hearty and filling, and because they're sweetened naturally by the bananas, you don't have to worry about a midmorning sugar crash. Prep the cookies on a Sunday to have an easy on-the-go breakfast throughout the week.

MAKES 8 COOKIES

- 2 ripe bananas
- 1 cup (105 g) cauliflower rice (see page 18)
- 2 large eggs
- ⅓ cup (85 g) natural peanut butter
- 2 cups (230 g) blanched almond flour (see Note)
- 1 teaspoon baking soda
- ¼ teaspoon sea salt
- ½ teaspoon ground cinnamon
- ⅓ cup (53 g) flax seeds
- ⅓ cup (53 g) raw sunflower seeds
- ⅓ cup (38 g) chopped raw pumpkin seeds
- ⅓ cup (38 g) chopped raw pecans
- ⅓ cup (54 g) dried cranberries
- ⅓ cup (58 g) mini dark chocolate chips
- Coarse sea salt for sprinkling on top

1. Preheat the oven to 350°F (180°C). Line a baking sheet with parchment paper.

2. In a large bowl, mash the bananas with a fork. Add the cauliflower rice, eggs, and peanut butter. Whisk together until well combined; the mixture will still be lumpy from the mashed bananas.

3. Add the almond flour, baking soda, salt, and cinnamon and use a rubber spatula to fold together until well combined.

4. In a small bowl, mix together the flax seeds, sunflower seeds, pumpkin seeds, pecans, cranberries, and chocolate chips, reserving some of the mix to sprinkle on top. Fold the remaining mixture into the cookie dough.

5. Use a small ice cream scoop or 2 spoons to scoop 8 mounds onto the prepared baking sheet (about 2 tablespoons of the mixture per mound), spacing them about 2 inches (5 cm) apart. Sprinkle some of the reserved dried fruit, nuts, seeds, and chocolate chips on top of each mound, pressing them gently into the top to flatten the cookies a bit. Bake for 17 to 20 minutes, until golden brown.

6. While the cookies are still warm, sprinkle with coarse sea salt. Allow the cookies to cool on the baking sheet for a couple of minutes to set before transferring to a cooling rack. The cookies will keep for up to 10 days in an airtight container in the fridge.

Note: Blanched almond flour is finer than almond meal and has a lighter beige color because the almond skins aren't ground up with the nuts when processed. While almond meal can be great for recipes that aim for a hearty consistency, when baking I tend to use blanched almond flour because it results in a lighter, smoother texture, and a more traditional pastry color.

CINNAMON-PECAN COFFEE CAKE

THIS COFFEE CAKE is a deliciously edible oxymoron. It's fluffy yet dense, crumbly yet moist, and sweet yet savory. Pair it with a simple dollop of whole-milk yogurt or serve it as part of a brunch menu with quiche (see page 72) and some Classic Vanilla Waffles (page 42). Want to take it up a notch to really wow your guests? Make the caramel sauce and drizzle it over the top.

SERVES 8

- 2 cups (270 g) cauliflower florets (see page 16)
- ½ cup (80 g) coconut sugar
- 4 tablespoons (½ stick/57 g) salted butter
- 1 teaspoon vanilla extract
- 2 large eggs
- 2 cups (230 g) blanched almond flour (see Note, page 31)
- 1½ teaspoons baking powder
- ½ teaspoon baking soda
- ½ teaspoon sea salt

FOR THE CINNAMON-PECAN TOPPING

- 1 cup (120 g) chopped pecans
- ¼ cup (30 g) blanched almond flour
- ¼ cup (40 g) coconut sugar
- 4 tablespoons (½ stick/57 g) salted butter, melted
- 1½ teaspoons ground cinnamon

- Caramel Sauce (optional; recipe follows)

1. Preheat the oven to 350°F (180°C). Line a 9 by 5-inch (22 by 13 cm) pan with parchment paper, leaving 2 long edges that extend beyond the pan's sides.

2. Bring an inch of water to a boil in a medium saucepan. Place the cauliflower in a steamer basket set over the boiling water. Cover and steam the florets for 5 minutes, until easily pierced with a fork.

3. Transfer the cooked florets to a food processor and process for 10 seconds, until all the florets are completely chopped into a meal (see page 19). Place the processed cauliflower in a clean, thin dish towel or piece of cheesecloth and set aside in a strainer for about 5 minutes, until it is cool enough to handle.

4. Meanwhile, in the bowl of a stand mixer or in a large bowl using a handheld electric mixer, cream together the coconut sugar, butter, and vanilla until light and fluffy, about 1 minute. Add the eggs and beat again until well combined.

5. Once the cauliflower meal is cool, gather the ends of the towel and squeeze as much liquid out of the cauliflower as possible. Removing excess liquid will ensure the cake won't be soggy. Add the squeezed cauliflower to the butter and sugar mixture and beat to combine.

CONTINUED

6. Add the almond flour to the bowl along with the baking powder, baking soda, and salt. Mix until completely combined.

7. Make the topping: In a small bowl, mix the pecans, almond flour, coconut sugar, butter, and cinnamon.

8. Pour half the batter into the prepared pan. Tap the bottom of the pan a couple of times on the counter to even out the batter and to remove any air bubbles. Sprinkle half of the cinnamon-pecan topping in an even layer on top of the batter and then pour the remaining batter over the top. Finish with the remaining topping.

9. Bake for 35 minutes, or until the center rises, the edges are golden brown, and a toothpick inserted in the center comes out clean. Allow the cake to cool in the pan for 5 minutes before pulling up the edges of the parchment paper to transfer the cake to a cooling rack. After 10 minutes, transfer to a cutting board and cut into 8 squares.

10. If using the caramel sauce, drizzle over the tops of the squares once they are plated.

11. Store in an airtight container in the fridge for up to a week.

CARAMEL SAUCE

MAKES ABOUT 1½ CUPS

- 1 13.5-ounce (398 mL) can unsweetened coconut cream (preferably Thai Kitchen or Native Forest brand)
- ½ cup (80 g) coconut sugar
- 1 teaspoon vanilla extract
- ½ teaspoon sea salt

1. Place the coconut cream and coconut sugar in a small pot over high heat and bring to a boil. Reduce the heat to medium and maintain the sauce at a simmer for about 20 minutes, whisking frequently, until it thickens. Remove from the heat and whisk in the vanilla and salt.

2. The sauce can be stored in a covered container in the fridge for up to 2 weeks and can be used as anything from an ice cream topper to a dip for apple slices.

CINNAMON-SUGAR BLUEBERRY MUFFINS

THESE SWEET AND cinnamony blueberry muffins are the perfect poppable treat whether you're enjoying them with your morning coffee or packing them in lunchboxes. Customize the flavor of these muffins with the seasons by swapping in the same amount of raspberries, strawberries, or apples in place of the blueberries.

MAKES 24 MINI MUFFINS OR 12 REGULAR MUFFINS

- 1½ cups (203 g) cauliflower florets (see page 16)
- 3 large eggs
- ⅓ cup (53 g) coconut sugar
- ⅓ cup (80 g) ghee, refined coconut oil, or unsalted butter
- 2 tablespoons agave nectar, honey, or maple syrup (see Note, page 25)
- 1 teaspoon of vanilla extract
- ½ teaspoon ground cinnamon
- 1 cup (115 g) blanched almond flour (see Note, page 31)
- 2 tablespoons tapioca flour
- 1 tablespoon baking powder
- ½ teaspoon sea salt
- 1¼ cups (170 g) fresh blueberries

1. Preheat the oven to 350°F (180°C). Line a muffin tin with paper liners.

2. Process the cauliflower florets in a food processor for about 30 seconds until they are completely chopped into a meal (see page 19). Transfer the meal to a microwave-safe bowl and microwave for 3 minutes. (Alternatively, you could steam the florets first, then transfer them to a food processor to chop into a meal.) Transfer the meal to the center of a clean, thin dish towel or piece of cheesecloth, set over a strainer, and let cool.

3. Rinse and dry the food processor (you'll use it again, so don't go into full cleaning mode).

4. Put the eggs, coconut sugar, ghee, agave nectar, vanilla, and cinnamon in the food processor and process until combined, about 10 seconds. Use a rubber spatula to scrape down the sides of the work bowl.

5. When the cauliflower meal is cool enough to handle, gather the corners of the towel, and working over the sink, squeeze out the excess liquid.

6. Measure out a packed ½ cup (57 g) of the squeezed cauliflower and add it to the food processor. If there is any excess cauliflower meal, it can be stored in an airtight container in the fridge for a week or frozen

for later use. If you have a little less than 1/2 cup (57 g), that's okay too. Process the wet ingredients again until well combined, about 10 seconds.

7. Add the almond flour, tapioca flour, baking powder, and salt to the wet ingredients in the food processor. Process for another 10 to 15 seconds, until the dry and wet ingredients are well combined.

8. Remove the blade of the food processor and fold in most of the blueberries, saving some for the top. You can also transfer the batter to a bowl to fold in the blueberries, but I like to avoid any extra dirty dishes.

9. Use a spoon to scoop the batter into the prepared muffin tin, filling each cup three-quarters full. If cups are overfilled, they will overflow when baking. Top each muffin with 2 or 3 blueberries.

10. Bake the muffins for 20 minutes, until the edges and top are golden brown and a toothpick poked in the center comes out clean.

11. Transfer to a cooling rack and allow to cool for 10 minutes before eating. The muffins will keep for up to 1 week in an airtight container in the fridge or in the freezer for up to 2 months.

CINNAMON CHOCOLATE SCONES

RICH DARK CHOCOLATE and cinnamon make these scones the perfect partner for your morning coffee or tea. Using cauliflower in the batter adds extra vitamins and minerals that are lacking in traditional flour scones. While the cauliflower and almond flour make for a substantial and filling scone, the tapioca flour brings a lightness to the mix. Swap out the chocolate for some blueberries or apple pieces to transform these treats with the season. ·

MAKES 12 SCONES

- 2 cups (270 g) cauliflower florets (see page 16)
- ⅓ cup plus 2 tablespoons (73 g) coconut sugar
- 2 large eggs
- ½ teaspoon vanilla bean powder (or 1 teaspoon vanilla extract)
- 3 cups (345 g) blanched almond flour (see Note, page 31)
- ⅔ cup (90 g) tapioca flour, plus more for the work surface
- 1 tablespoon baking powder
- ½ teaspoon sea salt, plus more for sprinkling
- 1½ teaspoons ground cinnamon
- 8 tablespoons (1 stick/113 g) unsalted butter, at room temperature
- ⅓ cup (58 g) 60% cacao dark chocolate, roughly chopped

1. Bring an inch of water to a boil in a medium saucepan. Place the cauliflower in a steamer basket set over the boiling water. Cover and steam the florets for about 5 minutes, until easily pierced with a fork.

2. Transfer the steamed florets to a high-powered blender with the ⅓ cup (53 g) coconut sugar, the eggs, and the vanilla bean powder. Blend on high for 1 minute, until the ingredients are thoroughly combined and the mixture is completely smooth. Set aside.

3. In a large bowl, whisk together 2 cups (230 g) of the almond flour, ⅓ cup (45 g) of the tapioca flour, the baking powder, salt, and cinnamon.

4. Cut the butter into small pieces and add them to the bowl. With your hands, knead the butter into the dry ingredients. The mixture will remain dry and crumbly, but knead the dough until the butter is evenly distributed and the mixture holds together when you squeeze it in the palm of your hand.

5. Pour the cauliflower mixture from the blender into the bowl with the dry ingredients. Use your hands to mix everything together. Add the remaining cup (115 g) of the almond flour and use your hands or a rubber spatula to fold it in to the dough. Once

combined, add the remaining ⅓ cup (45 g) of tapioca flour. Fold in the majority of the chocolate, reserving some chunks to put on top of the scones.

6. Place the dough in the freezer for 30 minutes. While it is chilling, preheat the oven to 400°F (200°C). Line a rimmed baking sheet with parchment paper.

7. Sprinkle a cutting board with tapioca flour. After 30 minutes, remove the dough from the freezer, set on the cutting board, and use a knife to cut the dough in half. With your hands, form each half into a circle. With a sharp knife, cut one of the circles into 6 even triangles. Use your hands to reshape the triangles, if needed, and place them on the prepared baking sheet about 1 to 2 inches (3 to 5 cm) apart. Repeat with the remaining dough.

8. Once all 12 triangles are on the baking sheet, press the remaining chopped chocolate into the tops of each scone. Sprinkle the scones with the remaining 2 tablespoons coconut sugar.

9. Bake for 20 to 25 minutes, until the tops of the scones are golden brown. Transfer to a rack to cool for about 5 minutes before enjoying.

10. The scones will keep in an airtight container in the fridge for about 10 days.

CLASSIC VANILLA WAFFLES

EVERYONE NEEDS A classic waffle recipe in their repertoire. Whether you're making waffles for a cozy weekend breakfast, throwing a scoop of ice cream on top for dessert à la mode, or pairing them with fried chicken for a Southern-style dinner, this recipe will not disappoint. The batter comes together in a blender so, unlike most waffle recipes, this one requires minimal prep and minimal cleanup. Adding cauliflower reduces the amount of liquids and oil/butter needed and ups the nutrient profile by contributing vitamin C, vitamin K, and HDL (aka the good cholesterol) among other benefits. Make flavored waffles by mixing in blueberries, chocolate chips, or pumpkin spice.

MAKES 4 WAFFLES

- 2 cups (270 g) cauliflower florets (see page 16)
- ½ cup (120 mL) whole milk
- ¼ cup (40 g) coconut sugar
- 1 large egg
- 1 teaspoon vanilla extract
- 1½ cups (172 g) blanched almond flour (see Note, page 31)
- ½ cup (85 g) cassava flour
- ½ cup (68 g) tapioca flour
- 1 tablespoon baking powder
- ¼ teaspoon sea salt
- Butter, for greasing the waffle iron and for serving
- Pure maple syrup (see Note, page 25), for serving
- Homemade Whipped Cream (optional; recipe follows)
- 2 cups fresh berries (optional)

1. Preheat a waffle iron. Preheat your oven to 200°F (90°C) or its lowest temperature.

2. Place the florets, milk, coconut sugar, egg, and vanilla in a high-powered blender. Blend on high until completely smooth and well combined, about 1 minute.

3. Add the almond flour, cassava flour, tapioca flour, baking powder, and salt to the blender and blend again on high for about 1 minute, until completely combined. You may need to take breaks to scrape down the sides of the blender.

4. Brush the waffle iron liberally with 1 tablespoon melted butter. Use a measuring cup to scoop ⅓ cup (80 mL) of batter into the waffle iron. Close it and cook until the waffle iron light goes off or the waffle appears golden brown and fluffy, about 5 minutes. Transfer the finished waffles to a baking sheet and keep them warm in the oven while you work through all of the batter.

5. Serve the waffles with butter and maple syrup. Alternatively, top with homemade whipped cream (recipe follows) and fresh berries.

HOMEMADE WHIPPED CREAM

**MAKES ABOUT 1 CUP
(240 ML)**

- ½ cup (120 mL) heavy cream
- 2 tablespoons maple syrup
  (see Note, page 25)
- 1 teaspoon vanilla extract
- Pinch of sea salt

Pour the cream into the bowl of a stand mixer or a bowl
for use with a handheld mixer. Whip on high for 3 minutes, until the cream begins to stiffen. Add the maple
syrup, vanilla, and salt. Continue to whip for another
3 minutes, until firm peaks form. Whipped cream keeps
in the fridge in an airtight container for about 1 week.

CAULIFLOWER FRENCH TOAST

CAULIFLOWER STEAKS CAN be transformed into sweet French toast. Coat them in egg and cassava flour—a gluten-free, grain-free, and nut-free flour made from yucca, a root vegetable. It's a higher-carb flour than a nut flour, so it gives the breading a more traditional texture. The almond flour adds an extra layer of flavor because it has more of a nutty, creamy taste (but you could use only cassava flour, if you prefer). To finish, serve the French toast with maple syrup and butter.

SERVES 4

- 4 cauliflower steaks, cut ½ inch (1.25 cm) thick and weighing 4¼ ounces/125 g each (17¼ ounces/500 g total), plus the remaining florets (see pages 15 and 16)
- ½ cup (85 g) cassava flour
- 2 large eggs
- ½ cup (57 g) blanched almond flour (see Note, page 31)
- ¼ cup (40 g) coconut sugar
- 1 teaspoon ground cinnamon
- ½ teaspoon sea salt
- 4 tablespoons (½ stick/57 g) salted butter, plus more for serving
- Maple syrup (see Note, page 25), for serving

1. Save the cauliflower that falls away from the head as you cut it into steaks and cut into medium florets.

2. Bring an inch of water to a boil in a deep saucepan. Set a steamer basket over the boiling water and arrange the steaks standing up in the basket with the florets around them. Cover and steam for 7 minutes, until the steaks are easily pierced with a fork.

3. Place the cassava flour in a shallow bowl wide enough to fit the steaks. Whisk the eggs in a second shallow bowl. Put the almond flour, coconut sugar, cinnamon, and salt in a third shallow bowl and stir to combine.

4. When the steaks and florets are tender, remove from the heat and let cool. One by one, place them in the cassava flour and flip to thoroughly coat both sides. Dip each steak and floret in the egg and then in the almond flour mixture, coating both sides. Set each breaded piece aside on a plate. Repeat this process until all the steaks and florets have been coated.

5. In a skillet wide enough to hold 2 of the steaks, melt 2 tablespoons of the butter over medium-high heat. Once the butter is melted and bubbling, reduce the heat to medium and place 2 steaks and some florets

in the pan, being careful not to crowd them. Flip after 2 to 3 minutes, when the underside is golden brown. Cook for another 2 to 3 minutes, until browned on the other side, and then transfer to a plate. Add more butter to the pan as needed and cook the remaining steaks and florets.

6. Serve immediately with butter and maple syrup.

1. Coat both sides of the cauliflower steak in cassava flour.

2. Dip the steak into the bowl with the beaten eggs; be sure to coat each side.

3. Place the steak into the almond flour mixture to "bread" each side.

4. Once both sides of the steak are coated, set it aside on a plate and repeat these steps until all the steaks are fully coated.

EVERYTHING BAGELS

YOU'LL LOVE THE doughy texture of these bagels and you can modify the toppings to mimic the flavor of your favorite bagels. Try the Everything Seasoning or use the components separately to make a bagel with all sesame seeds or all poppy seeds or all onion flakes instead. You can even make one of each for a bagel assortment.

MAKES 4 BAGELS, EACH ABOUT 4 INCHES (10 CM) IN DIAMETER

FOR THE BAGELS

- 2 cups (270 g) cauliflower florets (see page 16)
- 2 cups (230 g) blanched almond flour (see Note, page 31)
- ½ cup (67 g) tapioca flour
- 2 tablespoons cider vinegar
- 2 tablespoons agave nectar (see Note, page 25)
- 2 teaspoons baking powder
- 1 teaspoon sea salt
- 2 large egg yolks, whisked

FOR THE EVERYTHING SEASONING

- 2 teaspoons poppy seeds
- 1 teaspoon white sesame seeds
- 1 teaspoon black sesame seeds
- 1½ teaspoons dried onion flakes
- 1½ teaspoons dried garlic flakes

1. Preheat the oven to 350°F (180°C). Line a baking sheet with parchment paper.

2. Bring an inch of water to a boil in a medium saucepan. Place the cauliflower in a steamer basket set over the boiling water. Cover and steam for 5 minutes, until the florets are easily pierced with a fork. Transfer the steamed cauliflower to a food processor and process until the florets are completely chopped into a meal (see page 19).

3. Make the seasoning: In a small bowl, mix together the poppy seeds, white and black sesame seeds, onion flakes, and garlic flakes. Set aside.

4. Transfer the cauliflower meal to a clean, thin dish towel or piece of cheesecloth and let cool for a few minutes. Working over the sink, pull the corners of the towel together and squeeze out the excess liquid. Place the squeezed cauliflower meal in a large bowl along with the almond flour, tapioca flour, vinegar, agave nectar, baking powder, salt, and 2 teaspoons of the everything seasoning. Knead and fold the dough with your hands until it is completely combined and forms a large ball.

5. Divide the dough into 4 pieces using a sharp knife or pastry cutter. Using your hands, form the dough into discs a little bit larger than your palm (about 4 inches/10 cm in diameter and 1 inch/3 cm thick) and use your finger to poke a hole in the center.

CONTINUED

Reform and press the dough into a bagel shape if the bagel gets misshapen when you poke the hole.

6. Bring a medium pot of water to a boil, then reduce the heat to a simmer. Using your hands or a slotted spoon, place one bagel in the water. When the bagel floats to the top of the water, in about 30 seconds, flip it and continue to boil for another 30 seconds until the outside of the bagel looks soft and doughy. Use a slotted spoon to transfer the bagel from the boiling water to the prepared baking sheet. Repeat until all the bagels are boiled. Transfer the baking sheet to the oven and bake for 10 minutes, until the bagels just start to look toasty on the outside.

7. Remove the bagels from the oven, brush each one liberally with egg yolk, and sprinkle generously with the seasoning. Bake for another 20 minutes, until the bagels are cooked through and the tops are golden brown. The bagels don't expand too much and should be firm to the touch. Allow the bagels to rest for 10 minutes before serving.

8. Serve the bagels as is, to be pulled apart, cut in half, toasted, or topped with butter, cream cheese, sliced avocado, or your favorite bagel topping.

9. The bagels will keep in the fridge for about 10 days in an airtight container or can be wrapped individually in plastic wrap and frozen for up to 6 months.

CAULIFLOWER, PEPPER, AND QUINOA FRITTATAS

SAVORY FRITTATAS CAN be transformed into nutritious grab-and-go breakfasts. Not only are these single-serving frittatas loaded with essential vitamins and minerals from the cauliflower and spinach, but they also pack a protein punch. Quinoa is a great source of plant-based protein that will help keep you full all morning long.

MAKES 12 MUFFIN-SIZE FRITTATAS

- ½ cup (113 g) uncooked white quinoa (but any kind of quinoa works)
- 1 cup (240 mL) vegetable broth
- 2 tablespoons extra-virgin olive oil
- 1 red bell pepper, chopped
- 1 sweet onion, chopped
- 2 cups (270 g) coarsely chopped cauliflower florets (see page 16)
- 1 cup (28 g) chopped fresh spinach
- 1 cup (120 g) shredded Cheddar
- 3 tablespoons shredded Parmesan
- 4 large eggs
- ½ teaspoon dry mustard
- ½ teaspoon garlic powder
- ¼ teaspoon sea salt
- ¼ teaspoon freshly ground black pepper

1. Preheat the oven to 350°F (180°C). Line a 12-cup muffin pan with paper liners or spray with cooking spray.

2. Place the quinoa in a fine-mesh metal strainer and rinse it thoroughly. Combine the quinoa and vegetable broth in a medium pot over high heat. Bring to a boil, then cover and reduce to a simmer. Continue cooking for 15 to 20 minutes, until the quinoa is fluffy and has absorbed all the broth. Transfer to a large bowl.

3. While the quinoa is cooking, in a large skillet over medium-high heat, combine the olive oil, bell pepper, onion, and cauliflower and cook for 10 to 15 minutes, stirring occasionally, until the onion begins to caramelize and the cauliflower and peppers are browned.

4. Transfer the veggies to the bowl with the quinoa. Add the chopped spinach, Cheddar, Parmesan, eggs, dry mustard, garlic powder, salt, and pepper. Stir everything together until well combined.

5. Use a ⅓-cup (80 mL) measure to scoop the frittata mixture into the muffin cups. These don't expand much, so you can fill each cup to the top. Bake for about 25 minutes, until the centers are set and the edges are golden brown.

CONTINUED

6. Transfer the frittatas to a cooling rack. Enjoy immediately or wait for them to cool completely before storing in an airtight container in the fridge for up to a week. Reheat the frittatas in the microwave for about one minute or in an oven set at 350°F (180°C) for about 4 minutes.

EGGS IN A NEST

PUSH THE BOUNDARIES of the traditional "eggs in a hole" and let cauliflower become the perfect resting place for eggs. To make the nest, take the time to arrange the florets in a perfect circle and tuck smaller florets into any gaps. Crack an egg into the small center hole and let it cook until firm. Brightly colored purple, orange, or green cauliflower makes this dish especially pretty and festive, but any color of cauliflower works just as well.

SERVES 4

- 4 slices bacon
- 4 cups (540 g) small to medium cauliflower florets (see page 16)
- 4 tablespoons (60 mL) olive oil
- 1 teaspoon garlic powder
- ½ teaspoon onion powder
- ½ teaspoon ground cumin
- ½ teaspoon chipotle chili powder
- ¼ teaspoon sea salt
- ¼ teaspoon freshly ground black pepper
- 4 large eggs
- ⅓ cup (40 g) shredded Cheddar
- ⅓ cup (40 g) finely chopped red onion
- 1 tablespoon chopped fresh chives
- Red pepper flakes

1. Line a plate with a paper towel and set aside.

2. Place the bacon in a medium skillet over medium heat. Cook for 5 to 7 minutes, flipping frequently, until crispy on both sides. Transfer to the prepared plate. Once cool, place the bacon on a cutting board and coarsely chop into small pieces.

3. Bring an inch of water to a boil in a medium saucepan. Place the cauliflower in a steamer basket set over the boiling water. Cover and steam the florets for about 5 minutes, until easily pierced with a fork.

4. Place the steamed florets in a large bowl. Toss with 2 tablespoons of the olive oil and the garlic powder, onion powder, cumin, chipotle chili powder, salt, and pepper.

5. Heat 1 tablespoon olive oil in a 12-inch (30 cm) skillet over medium-high heat. Add the florets to the pan and cook for 7 minutes, stirring occasionally, until golden brown. Once browned, return the cauliflower to the large bowl.

6. Wipe out the pan (or grab a clean skillet), place it over medium heat, and pour in the last tablespoon of olive oil. Once the oil starts to glisten, reduce the heat to medium-low. For each nest, arrange the cauliflower florets in a circle with the stems facing in and the florets facing out (fit as many as you can without crowding the

pan; you should be able to fit at least 2 nests). Carefully crack an egg into the center of the nest. If the cauliflower separates at any part of the nest, fill the gap with smaller florets. Cook until the egg whites are set and the yolks are runny, about 4 minutes.

7. While the eggs are cooking, sprinkle about 1 tablespoon each of cheese and red onion around the edges of each nest, avoiding the center yolk.

8. When the egg whites are cooked through, use a spatula to transfer the nests to plates. Sprinkle with the chopped bacon, chives, and red pepper flakes. Enjoy immediately.

CAULIFLOWER "BACON" BITS

THE KEY TO creating a convincing replacement for delicious but not-so-healthy bacon is patience: you need to roast cauliflower rice until it reaches a crunchy yet chewy texture. Keep the "bacon" bits in a jar in your fridge to sprinkle on your avocado toast or over your eggs every morning. Then reach back into the fridge to sprinkle them on your lunchtime salad. You'll find yourself using these bits on everything, and I can't blame you if you want to eat them straight from the jar.

MAKES ABOUT 1 CUP

- 3 cups (315 g) cauliflower rice (see page 18)
- 1 tablespoon soy sauce or tamari
- 1 tablespoon liquid smoke (see Note)
- 1 tablespoon coconut sugar
- ¼ teaspoon smoked paprika
- ¼ teaspoon garlic powder
- ⅛ teaspoon sea salt
- ⅛ teaspoon freshly ground black pepper

1. Preheat the oven to 275°F (135°C). Line a rimmed baking sheet with parchment paper.

2. Spread the cauliflower rice out on the prepared pan. Bake for 1 hour. Use a spatula to toss the rice and spread again in an even layer. Bake for another 20 minutes. Once the texture is sticky and dehydrated, turn off the oven, open the door a couple of inches, and allow the cauliflower to come to room temperature in the oven, about 30 minutes.

3. In a medium bowl, combine the soy sauce, liquid smoke, coconut sugar, paprika, garlic powder, salt, and pepper. Once the rice is cooled and crunchy, add it to the bowl and toss until the rice is completely coated.

4. Preheat the oven again to 275°F (135°C) and replace the parchment paper on the baking sheet.

5. Spread the coated cauliflower rice back on the lined baking sheet. Bake for 10 minutes, then turn off the oven. Open the oven door a couple inches and leave the bits in the oven for 5 to 10 minutes to cool.

6. Store the bits in an airtight container in the fridge for up to 2 weeks.

Note: Liquid smoke is often used with barbecue spices and rubs to give foods a rich, smoky flavor. Find it in your local grocery store near the ketchup and barbecue sauces.

CAULIFLOWER TOTS

WITHOUT SKIMPING ON any flavor, cauliflower stands in for the traditional tater in these tots. They're a lower-carb, lower-calorie, and nutrient-packed alternative to potatoes. Although traditional tots don't typically have cheese, the shredded Parmesan and Cheddar not only add flavor but also help hold the tots together. Want to make them dairy free? Shredded dairy-free cheese (try brands like Daiya, So Delicious, and Follow Your Heart) can be subbed 1:1 for traditional shredded cheese. Serve these tots with your morning eggs alongside some Cauliflower "Bacon" Bits (page 58).

MAKES 34 TOTS

- 4 cups (540 g) cauliflower florets (see page 16)
- 1 large egg
- ½ onion, grated
- ¼ cup (30 g) shredded Parmesan
- ¼ cup (30 g) shredded Cheddar
- ¼ cup (30 g) blanched almond flour (see Note, page 31)
- Sea salt and freshly ground black pepper
- Avocado oil cooking spray
- Ketchup, for serving (optional)

1. Preheat the oven to 400°F (200°C). Line a rimmed baking sheet with parchment paper.

2. Bring an inch of water to a boil in a medium saucepan. Place the cauliflower in a steamer basket set over the boiling water. Cover and steam the florets for 5 minutes, until they're easily pierced with a fork.

3. Working in batches, place the steamed florets in the food processor and process for 10 seconds until they are completely chopped into a meal (see page 19). Transfer each batch of meal to a clean, thin dish towel or piece of cheesecloth. Continue to process the remaining florets. Once all the cauliflower meal is cool enough to handle, gather the corners of the towel and, working over the sink, squeeze out as much liquid as you can. Transfer the squeezed meal to a large bowl.

4. Add the egg, grated onion, Parmesan and Cheddar cheeses, almond flour, and salt and pepper to taste to the bowl with the cauliflower. Use a rubber spatula to mix everything together. Allow the mixture to rest for 5 minutes so it can come together.

5. Spray the prepared baking sheet generously with cooking spray. Use your hands to form 34 small "tater" tots, about 1 inch (3 cm) long by ½ inch (1 cm) wide, placing them on the baking sheet about 1 inch

(3 cm) apart. All the tots should fit on one pan, though you can work in batches if needed. Spray the tots generously with cooking spray.

6. Bake for about 20 minutes, until golden brown. Flip the tots and continue to cook for another 10 minutes, until they are browned all over.

7. While the tots are hot, sprinkle with additional salt and serve with ketchup, if desired.

8. Any leftover tots can be stored in an airtight container in the fridge for 10 days. To reheat, place the tots on a baking sheet and broil them on high for a couple of minutes until heated through and crispy on the outside.

SPICY WAFFLED HASH BROWNS

....

MAKING HASH BROWNS on a waffle iron is a nontraditional (and ingenious) use for this kitchen tool. The waffle iron cooks the hash browns with crisp nooks and crannies that make for the perfect crunch. Think of the hash browns as a flavorful and nutritious vehicle to load up with your favorite breakfast foods. Use the hash brown as a base for some sliced avocado, bacon, and a sunny-side-up egg. Or, add a second hash brown on top for a breakfast sandwich. To make a Mexi-version, top a hash brown with eggs, sour cream, salsa, and beans.

SERVES 6

- 4 cups (540 g) cauliflower florets (page 16)
- 1¼ cups (150 g) shredded Mexican cheese blend
- ½ cup (60 g) blanched almond flour (see Note, page 31)
- ½ onion, grated
- ½ cup (79 g) fresh or frozen and thawed corn kernels
- ¼ cup (10 g) chopped fresh cilantro leaves
- 2 large eggs
- 1 jalapeño (seeds and stem removed), finely chopped
- 1 teaspoon baking powder
- 1 teaspoon ground cumin
- ½ teaspoon smoked paprika
- ¼ teaspoon chipotle chili powder
- ¼ teaspoon sea salt
- ¼ teaspoon freshly ground black pepper

(continued)

1. Preheat the waffle iron. Preheat the oven to its lowest temperature to keep the hash browns warm as you work through the batter.

2. Bring an inch of water to a boil in a medium saucepan. Place the cauliflower in a steamer basket set over the boiling water. Cover and steam the florets for 5 minutes, until easily pierced with a fork. Transfer the florets to a food processor and process until completely chopped into a meal (see page 19).

3. Transfer the meal to a clean, thin dish towel or piece of cheesecloth. Let cool. Working over the sink, pull the corners of the towel together and squeeze out the excess liquid. Place the squeezed meal in a large bowl.

4. Add 1 cup (120 g) of the cheese, the almond flour, onion, corn, cilantro, eggs, jalapeño, baking powder, cumin, paprika, chili powder, salt, and pepper to the bowl. Stir everything together until well combined.

5. Brush the waffle iron with melted butter to thoroughly grease it. Scoop ½ cup (120 mL) of the hash brown mixture into the waffle iron, spreading it out to an even layer. Close the iron and cook for 7 to 10 minutes, or until the waffle iron light indicates the hash

- Melted butter, for greasing the waffle iron and skillet

OPTIONAL TOPPINGS

- 6 large eggs
- 1 avocado, sliced
- Cilantro leaves, for garnish
- Ketchup, for serving
- Salsa, for serving
- Sour cream, for serving
- Black beans, for serving

browns are cooked through and they are golden and crispy on the outside. Transfer to a baking sheet and keep warm in the oven while you cook the remaining hash browns.

6. While the last of the hash browns are cooking, heat a tablespoon of butter in a skillet over medium-high heat and crack a few eggs into the pan. Cook the eggs for 5 minutes, until the edges are a little crispy, the whites are set, and the yolks are still runny. Repeat until all the eggs are cooked.

7. Serve each hash brown with a fried egg, a few slices of avocado, and the remaining cheese. Garnish with cilantro. Consider offering ketchup, salsa, sour cream, and black beans as additional toppings.

CAULIFLOWER AND SWEET POTATO HASH

ADDING A VARIETY of vegetables to a traditional potato hash is not only a smart way to get your daily serving, but also a great way to use up any leftover produce you have in your fridge. I prefer the flavor of sweet potato over traditional potatoes, but you can use either. Leave the skin on the sweet potatoes for the added texture (but you can peel them if you must). The cauliflower florets easily take on the flavors of the onion and sausage. Pair this hash with fried eggs to make an especially satisfying morning meal.

SERVES 4

- 2 tablespoons extra-virgin olive oil
- 4 cups (540 g) cauliflower florets (see page 16)
- 1 sweet onion, coarsely chopped
- 1 medium sweet potato, cut into ½-inch (1 cm) cubes
- 1 pound (454 g) ground pork breakfast sausage
- 3 or 4 large eggs
- 1 cup (120 g) shredded pepper Jack
- Fresh basil, for garnish (optional)

1. Preheat the broiler to high.

2. Heat olive oil in a large, ovenproof skillet over medium-high heat. Once hot, add the cauliflower florets, onion, and sweet potato to the skillet. Cook for 10 to 15 minutes, stirring frequently, until the florets begin to brown and the onion begins to caramelize.

3. Add the pork to the skillet using a spatula to break it apart. Continue to cook for another 5 minutes, until the pork is browned and completely cooked through.

4. Reduce the heat to medium-low. Use the back of a wooden spoon to make 3 or 4 shallow depressions in the hash (depending on how many eggs you're using). Crack an egg into each depression and cook for about 5 minutes, until the egg whites are set.

5. Sprinkle the shredded cheese on top of the hash and transfer the skillet to the oven. Broil on high for about 2 minutes, until the whites of the eggs are fully cooked but the yolks are still runny.

6. Garnish with basil, if using. Hash is best eaten immediately, but leftovers can be kept in the fridge for about 5 days in an airtight container.

GARLIC-PARMESAN CAULIFLOWER TOAST

MOVE OVER AVOCADO toast—perfectly roasted cauliflower steaks are the ideal base for loading up with your favorite breakfast toppings, from eggs and greens to ricotta and jam.

SERVES 4

- 4 cauliflower steaks, cut ½ inch thick (see page 15)
- 3 tablespoons avocado oil
- 2 garlic cloves, minced
- ¼ teaspoon sea salt
- ¼ cup (30 g) shredded Parmesan
- 4 large eggs
- Handful of microgreens or fresh herbs
- 1 tablespoon black sesame seeds
- 1 tablespoon hemp hearts
- Hot sauce or ketchup, for serving (optional)

1. Preheat the oven to 400°F (200°C). Line a baking sheet with parchment paper. Position one rack in the middle of the oven and another beneath the broiler.

2. Place the cauliflower steaks on the prepared baking sheet and arrange any leftover florets around them.

3. In a small bowl, mix 2 tablespoons of the avocado oil with the garlic and sea salt. Brush both sides of the steaks and the florets with the oil mixture and sprinkle the edges of each steak with Parmesan, using about half of the cheese.

4. Roast the steaks for 15 minutes, until the tops are golden brown. Flip the steaks and the larger florets and sprinkle the outer edges of the cauliflower with the remaining Parmesan. Continue roasting for another 15 minutes, or until slightly browned. Turn the broiler on high and place the cauliflower toasts 6 inches from the heat source. Broil for about 2 minutes, until the edges turn crispy and golden brown.

5. While the cauliflower is broiling, fry the eggs. Heat the remaining 1 tablespoon avocado oil in a large skillet over medium-high heat. Crack 4 eggs into the pan (1 egg per steak). After about 3 minutes, or once the edges of the eggs begin to crisp, reduce the heat and continue to cook until the egg whites are no longer translucent.

6. Top each cauliflower steak with a sunny-side-up egg, a few microgreens, and a sprinkle of sesame seeds and hemp hearts. Serve with hot sauce or ketchup, if desired.

CHICKPEA AND FETA SHAKSHUKA

SHAKSHUKA IS A Middle Eastern dish of eggs poached in spicy tomato sauce. The cauliflower florets and chickpeas make this version heartier than a typical shakshuka. Serve with a piece of crusty bread to dip into the egg and to scoop up all the delicious, flavorful sauce.

SERVES 4

- 2 tablespoons extra-virgin olive oil
- 2 cups (270 g) small to medium cauliflower florets (see page 16)
- ¾ cup finely chopped red onion
- 1 15-ounce (425 g) can chickpeas, drained and rinsed
- 2 garlic cloves, minced
- 1 28-ounce (794 g) can fire-roasted crushed tomatoes
- 1 teaspoon smoked paprika
- 1 teaspoon ground cumin
- ¼ teaspoon red pepper flakes
- ¼ teaspoon sea salt
- ¼ teaspoon saffron
- 4 large eggs
- ¼ cup (10 g) fresh flat-leaf parsley leaves, chopped
- ½ cup (75 g) crumbled feta
- 4 slices of your favorite hearty bread, toasted

1. Preheat the broiler to high. Position a rack about 6 inches from the heat source.

2. Heat the olive oil in a large ovenproof skillet over medium-high heat. Add the cauliflower florets and ½ cup (60 g) of the red onion to the skillet. Reduce the heat to medium and cook for 10 minutes, stirring occasionally, until the onion caramelizes and the florets are browned. Add the chickpeas and garlic and cook for another 3 to 5 minutes, until the chickpeas are warmed through.

3. Add the tomatoes, ½ cup (120 mL) water, the paprika, cumin, pepper flakes, salt, and saffron. Stir together. Once the mixture begins to bubble, reduce the heat to medium-low. Simmer for about 7 minutes, until the sauce starts to thicken up.

4. Use a wooden spoon to create 4 shallow depressions in the mixture and crack one egg into each depression. Continue to cook on the stovetop for 3 minutes, then place the skillet under the broiler for about 2 minutes, until the egg whites are fully cooked.

5. Remove from the oven and sprinkle the parsley, remaining red onion, and feta on top. Serve with toasted bread.

CAULIFLOWER, FIG JAM, AND CARAMELIZED ONION QUICHE

QUICHE IS A dish perfect for any gathering. Here cauliflower—along with eggs, milk, and cheese—is the filling for an almond flour crust. A thin layer of fig jam adds a sweetness to the rich flavors. Keep your florets smaller for easier bites, but take the time to stand them upright for a prettier presentation. The almond flour crust is really versatile and can be filled with anything from chocolate ganache to pumpkin pie filling.

SERVES 8

FOR THE CRUST

- 4 tablespoons (½ stick/57 g) salted butter, room temperature or melted
- 2 large eggs
- 1 cup (115 g) blanched almond flour (see Note, page 31)
- ½ teaspoon sea salt

FOR THE FILLING

- 4 cups (540 g) small to medium purple cauliflower florets (any color will work; see page 16)
- 1 tablespoon salted butter
- 1 sweet onion cut into 3-inch (8-cm) pieces
- 3 tablespoons fig jam (see Note)
- 4 large eggs
- 1 large egg yolk
- 1 cup (240 mL) whole milk or heavy cream
- 1¼ cups (150 g) shredded Gruyère
- ¼ teaspoon sea salt

1. Preheat the oven to 350°F (180°C).

2. Make the crust: In a medium bowl, fold together the butter, 1 egg, the almond flour, and salt until combined. Place the bowl in the fridge and chill the dough for 30 minutes. If chilling for longer than 2 hours, cover the bowl or wrap the dough in plastic wrap to keep it fresh.

3. Dampen your hands to make it easier to work with the crust. Transfer the dough to a pie pan and use your hands to spread it across the bottom and up the sides. The crust is a lot more forgiving and malleable than a traditional piecrust, so really work it into an even layer. You can use your fingers to pinch a pattern all the way around the edge of the dough if you'd like to create a wavy crust.

4. Whisk the other egg in a small bowl. Brush the entire crust with the whisked egg.

5. Bake the crust for 12 to 15 minutes, until it just starts to turn golden brown. Set aside.

6. Make the filling: Bring an inch of water to a boil in a medium saucepan. Place the florets in a steamer basket set over the boiling water. Cover and steam for 3 minutes. Remove from the heat, uncover, and set aside.

CONTINUED

7. Heat the butter in a medium skillet over medium-low heat. Add the onion and cook, stirring occasionally, until browned and caramelized, 15 to 20 minutes.

8. Spread an even layer of fig jam across the bottom of the cooked crust.

9. In a large bowl, whisk together the caramelized onion, eggs and egg yolk, milk, and 1 cup (120 g) of the cheese. Pour this mixture into the crust, on top of the fig jam.

10. Arrange the florets on top of the quiche, with the stems facing down and the florets facing up. Sprinkle the top with the remaining cheese and sea salt.

11. Bake for 50 minutes, then broil on high for 2 minutes if the center is not yet golden brown. Allow the quiche to stand for 10 minutes before cutting into it. Leftovers can be stored in an airtight container in the fridge for about 5 days. Leftovers can be reheated in the microwave for about 1 minute or in the oven at 350°F (180°C) for about 5 minutes.

Note: Find fig jam in the cheese section of your local grocery store.

LUNCH

LUNCH IS AN easy time to incorporate more cauliflower into your daily diet. You can roast florets for a flavor-packed salad or transform the vegetable completely by turning it into mayonnaise or a garlicky dressing or even a lightened carbonara sauce. Use cauliflower rice to update a rainbow roll or transform your regular sandwich bread into a superhealthy seeded loaf. These lunches will leave you fully satisfied and nourish your body so you don't fall victim to the midafternoon slump.

MEDITERRANEAN SALAD

WITH KALE PESTO

....

SALADS THAT DON'T actually have any leafy greens are my favorite types of salad. You could eat this salad straight from the bowl, tucked inside a wrap, between two slices of bread, or, yes, on a bed of leafy greens.

SERVES 4

FOR THE SALAD

- 1 cup (165 g) canned chickpeas, drained and rinsed
- 1 cup (165 g) oil-packed artichoke hearts from a jar, drained and quartered
- ¾ cup (109 g) oil-packed sun-dried tomatoes, drained and coarsely chopped
- 1 tablespoon avocado oil
- 3 cups (405 g) orange cauliflower florets (or any color you can find) (see page 16)
- ½ cup (71 g) crumbled goat cheese

FOR THE KALE PESTO

- ¾ cup (94 g) pine nuts
- 2 cups (130 g) coarsely chopped curly kale, stems discarded
- ⅓ cup (80 mL) extra-virgin olive oil
- ¼ cup (30 g) shredded Parmesan
- 2 garlic cloves, minced
- ½ teaspoon sea salt

1. In a large bowl, combine the chickpeas, artichoke hearts, and sun-dried tomatoes.

2. In a large skillet, heat the avocado oil over medium-high heat. When the oil is hot, add the cauliflower florets to the pan. Sauté the cauliflower, stirring often, until the florets are browned and cooked through, about 10 minutes. Add the cauliflower to the bowl with the chickpeas.

3. While the cauliflower is cooking, toast the pine nuts for the pesto. Place the pine nuts in a small skillet over medium heat and shake the pan every minute. Once the pine nuts become fragrant, shake the pan almost constantly until the nuts are golden brown on both sides. Transfer the pine nuts to a small bowl.

4. Make the pesto: Combine ½ cup (63 g) of the toasted pine nuts, the kale, olive oil, Parmesan, garlic, and salt in a food processor. Pulse the pesto ingredients about five times. Use a rubber spatula to scrape down the sides and pulse again until smooth (or desired consistency) and all the ingredients are incorporated.

5. Add the pesto to the bowl with the chickpeas and cauliflower and fold everything together until the salad ingredients are nicely coated with the pesto.

6. Top with the crumbled goat cheese and remaining pine nuts and enjoy. Store leftovers in an airtight container in the fridge for up to 1 week.

CILANTRO-LIME CHICKPEA PASTA SALAD

I LOVE USING chickpea pasta because it's packed with protein and has all the same comforting goodness you get from traditional pasta. Experiment—whether you use traditional spaghetti, lentil spirals, edamame macaroni, or black bean noodles—this salad works with all of them.

SERVES 4

FOR THE PASTA SALAD

- 8 ounces (227 g) chickpea pasta
- 4 slices (4 ounces/113 g) prosciutto
- 1 tablespoon avocado oil
- 4 cups (540 g) small purple cauliflower florets (see page 16)
- 2 ounces (56 g) honey goat cheese

FOR THE CILANTRO-LIME PESTO

- 1 cup (40 g) fresh cilantro leaves
- ½ cup (45 g) sliced almonds
- ¼ cup (60 mL) avocado oil
- 1 tablespoon lime juice
- 1 tablespoon fresh mint leaves
- 2 garlic cloves, minced
- ¼ teaspoon sea salt

1. Cook the pasta according to package directions. Drain and set aside.

2. While the pasta is cooking, fry the prosciutto in a large skillet over medium-high heat for 5 minutes, flipping frequently until browned. Transfer to a plate and set aside.

3. In the same pan you used for the prosciutto, heat the avocado oil over medium-high heat and add the cauliflower florets. Cook for 10 minutes, stirring occasionally, until the florets are golden brown.

4. Meanwhile, make the pesto: Place the cilantro, almonds, avocado oil, lime juice, mint, garlic, and salt in a food processor and process for 10 seconds. Scrape down the sides and continue to process until all the ingredients are smooth and well combined.

5. Return the pasta to the pot it was cooked in. Add the cauliflower and pesto and mix until all the ingredients are coated with the pesto. Transfer to a serving dish.

6. Coarsely chop the crispy prosciutto and sprinkle it on top of the noodles. Crumble the goat cheese over all and dig in. This is best served warm, but it will keep in an airtight container in the fridge for about 5 days. Leftovers can be eaten chilled or reheated in the microwave or in a skillet. Add a tablespoon of water or oil to the pan, if needed, to thin the pesto.

ARUGULA AND ROASTED VEGGIE SALAD

WITH LEMON-CHIA DRESSING

....

I'M A STRONG believer that we eat with our eyes first, so whenever I see a rare color of one of my favorite vegetables, I have to try it. Orange cauliflower is a striking visual contrast to the green Brussels sprouts, but the recipe will work just as well with purple or traditional white cauliflower, so use what you can find. The zesty lemon-chia dressing tops off this flavorful light lunch.

SERVES 2 AS A MAIN COURSE, OR 4 AS A SIDE

FOR THE SALAD

- 5 cups (675 g) orange cauliflower florets (see page 16)
- 1 pound (454 g) Brussels sprouts, ends trimmed, sliced lengthwise
- 2 tablespoons avocado oil
- 1 tablespoon agave nectar, honey, or maple syrup (see Note, page 25)
- ¼ teaspoon sea salt
- 1 cup (40 g) arugula
- 1 cup (88 g) thinly sliced purple cabbage
- ¼ cup (38 g) chopped pistachios

FOR THE LEMON-CHIA DRESSING

- ¼ cup (60 mL) avocado oil
- Grated zest and juice of 1 lemon
- 1 tablespoon agave nectar, honey, or maple syrup
- 1 tablespoon white wine vinegar
- 2 teaspoons chia seeds or poppy seeds

1. Preheat the oven to 400°F (200°C). Line a baking sheet with parchment paper.

2. Toss the cauliflower florets and Brussels sprouts in a large bowl with the avocado oil, agave nectar, and salt.

3. Transfer the vegetables to the prepared baking sheet and roast for 30 minutes, until the vegetables are softened and just starting to brown. Then broil on high for 2 minutes to crisp the outsides of the vegetables.

4. While the vegetables are cooking, make the dressing: In a small Mason jar, combine the avocado oil, lemon zest and juice, agave nectar, vinegar, and chia seeds and shake well.

5. Arrange the arugula and cabbage on a platter. Place the cauliflower and Brussels sprouts on top of the greens and drizzle with the dressing.

6. Top with the pistachios and serve. I like to make the salad right before I'm going to eat it, but it will last a few days in the fridge. Bring leftover salad to room temperature before serving.

KALE CAESAR SALAD

WITH SMOKED CHICKPEA CROUTONS

KALE CAESAR IS the salad to make for your friend who says she hates kale. The creamy, cheesy dressing is enough to get even an avowed kale hater to finish her plate. I almost died from excitement when I first tasted this Caesar dressing made from cauliflower. It is so rich and decadent, even kale salad critics will approve.

SERVES 4

FOR THE DRESSING

- 2 cups (270 g) cauliflower florets (see page 16)
- ½ cup (60 g) shredded Parmesan
- ¼ cup (60 mL) extra-virgin olive oil
- Juice of 1 lemon
- 3 garlic cloves, minced
- 1 tablespoon Dijon mustard
- ⅛ teaspoon sea salt
- ⅛ teaspoon freshly ground black pepper

FOR THE SMOKED CHICKPEA CROUTONS

- 1 15-ounce (425 g) can chickpeas, drained and rinsed
- 1 tablespoon extra-virgin olive oil
- 1 teaspoon garlic powder
- 1 teaspoon smoked paprika
- 1 teaspoon sea salt

1. Bring an inch of water to a boil in a medium saucepan. Place the florets in a steamer basket set over the boiling water. Cover and steam for about 5 minutes, until they're easily pierced with a fork.

2. In a high-powdered blender, combine the cooked cauliflower with the Parmesan, olive oil, lemon juice, garlic, mustard, salt, and pepper. Blend on high speed for 2 minutes, until the dressing is completely smooth and combined. The dressing will be warm because of the steamed cauliflower. Transfer the dressing to an airtight container and refrigerate for an hour.

3. While the dressing is chilling, make the croutons: Preheat the oven to 400°F (200°C). Line a baking sheet with parchment.

4. In a large bowl, combine the chickpeas with the olive oil, garlic powder, smoked paprika, and salt. Toss until coated. Spread the chickpeas out on the prepared baking sheet and roast for 20 minutes. Check on the chickpeas after 10 minutes and shake the pan to toss them. The chickpeas should start to turn golden brown on the bottoms.

FOR THE SALAD

- 5 cups (105 g) coarsely chopped curly kale, stems discarded

- ½ cup (60 g) shaved Parmesan

5. Place the chopped kale in a large bowl. Drizzle with the Caesar dressing and toss until the kale leaves are completely coated. Top with the chickpea croutons and shaved Parmesan. Enjoy immediately. Any leftovers can be stored in an airtight container in the fridge for up to 2 days.

CALIFORNIA ROLL

WITH CAULIFLOWER STICKY RICE

. . . .

KEEPING NORI SHEETS on hand makes it easy to whip up a quick lunch. You can roll up nori with whatever you have in the fridge: shrimp, cooked sweet potato, fresh mango, or sushi-grade tuna. These rolls gave me the epiphany to try making cauliflower sticky rice, and it's the easiest (and tidiest) way to keep the rice and all the fillings tucked inside the nori sheet. If you love sticky rice but don't eat gelatin, see the vegan version in the Variation.

SERVES 2

- 3 cups (315 g) cauliflower rice (see page 18)
- 1 tablespoon seasoned rice vinegar
- 1 tablespoon powdered gelatin
- ¼ teaspoon sea salt
- 2 sheets of nori
- ¼ cup (32 g) crab, shrimp, or kani crab sticks
- ½ English cucumber, peeled (optional) and cut into 2-inch (5 cm) matchsticks
- 1 avocado, sliced
- Soy sauce, for serving
- Wasabi paste, for serving
- Pickled ginger (optional), for serving

1. In a medium skillet, cook the cauliflower rice over medium-high heat for about 5 minutes, stirring frequently. It will release a lot of steam. Once the steam dies down a bit, add the rice vinegar and stir for 30 seconds.

2. While stirring, sprinkle the gelatin across the entire pan of rice so that it doesn't all clump in one area. Add the salt and stir to combine. Heat the rice for another 2 minutes, stirring frequently.

3. Remove the pan from the heat and let cool to room temperature, about 1 hour. Immediately after cooking the rice may appear wet and shiny, but as it comes to room temperature it will congeal and resemble sticky rice.

4. Once the rice has cooled, lay a square nori sheet flat on a cutting board with the smooth side of the nori facing down. Place half of the sticky rice in the center of the sheet. Dampen your hands to keep the rice from sticking to them, and spread the rice across the sheet, stopping about 1 inch (3 cm) from the edge farthest from you. The edge without rice will be where you finish the roll.

5. Place half the crab, half of the cucumber sticks, and half the avocado on the side closest to you. Starting

with this side, tightly roll the nori until you get to the final edge you left free from rice.

6. Dip your finger in water and wet the last inch (3 cm) of nori. Press this edge onto the roll so that it sticks to the rolled nori. Repeat this process with the second nori sheet.

7. Use a sharp knife to cut each roll in half; then cut each half into 4 pieces. Each roll yields 8 pieces. Eat immediately with soy sauce, wasabi, and pickled ginger, if desired.

VARIATION

To make sticky rice without gelatin, try mixing the cauliflower rice with mashed avocado. Prep the cauliflower rice as described. After you stir in the rice vinegar, transfer the rice to a bowl. Mash half a ripe avocado and mix it in to create a creamy avocado-coated rice that is perfectly spreadable on your nori sheets. Roll up the remaining ingredients and continue as directed.

1. With damp hands, spread the cauliflower rice across the nori sheet, stopping about 1 inch (3 cm) from the far edge.

2. Add half the crab to the side of the sheet closest to you.

3. Place half the cucumber and avocado alongside the crab.

4. Starting at the side of the sheet with the crab, cucumber, and avocado, tightly roll the nori until you get to the final edge that is free of rice.

RAW RAINBOW PEANUT ROLL

....

THIS RAINBOW ROLL is packed with colorful raw veggies and is so flavorful that you'll completely forget you're having a "healthy lunch." Aside from the amazing crunch factor, it includes a creamy peanut sauce that absolutely makes the roll. Green leaf lettuce is a great choice for the outer wrap because it's super flexible and easy to roll. Switch it up and use a collard green leaf for a larger rainbow roll.

SERVES 4

FOR THE PEANUT SAUCE

- ¼ cup (64 g) natural peanut butter
- 2 tablespoons soy sauce or tamari
- 2 tablespoons agave nectar, honey, or maple syrup (see Note, page 25)
- 2 teaspoons toasted sesame oil

FOR THE ROLLS

- 8 large leaves of green leaf lettuce
- 3 cups (315 g) orange cauliflower rice (see page 18)
- 1 tablespoon chopped fresh mint leaves
- 4 cups (400 g) thinly sliced and coarsely chopped purple cabbage
- 1 red bell pepper, cut into thin strips
- ½ English cucumber, cut into thin strips
- ¼ cup (35 g) chopped roasted peanuts

1. Make the sauce: In a small bowl, whisk together the peanut butter, soy sauce, agave nectar, and sesame oil.

2. Assemble the rolls: Lay a lettuce leaf on a flat surface. Spread 2 tablespoons of the peanut sauce across the center of the leaf.

3. Sprinkle 2 tablespoons of the cauliflower rice and some of the mint on top of the peanut sauce.

4. Add some purple cabbage on top of the rice. Lay the pepper and cucumber slices crosswise, across the center of the leaf.

5. Fold the leaf, starting at the bottom and firmly tucking in the edges as you roll. Secure with toothpicks. Repeat with the remaining lettuce leaves until all the sauce and ingredients are used up.

6. When ready to eat, cut vertically across the center of the roll and sprinkle with chopped peanuts. Enjoy immediately or store ingredients separately in an airtight container in the fridge and assemble the roll just before eating. The ingredients keep for about 5 days.

CAULIFLOWER FALAFEL

FALAFEL CAN BE a canvas for many flavors. But this recipe is not just about adding new flavors to falafel. Instead, the traditional chickpeas are replaced with cooked cauliflower florets. For lunch, have this falafel on top of a salad with some roasted sweet potatoes, beets, and toasted nuts. For a group, it's fun to make a falafel bar and let your diners assemble their own pita sandwiches with everything from tomatoes and cucumbers to cooked quinoa.

MAKES 12; SERVES 4

- 2 tablespoons avocado oil
- 3⅓ cups (454 g) small cauliflower florets (see page 16)
- ½ sweet onion, cut into large pieces
- 2 garlic cloves
- ¼ cup (57 g) arrowroot flour (see Note)
- ¼ cup (29 g) blanched almond flour (see Note, page 31)
- 3 tablespoons fresh parsley leaves
- 1 teaspoon ground coriander
- 1 teaspoon ground cumin
- 1 large egg
- ¼ teaspoon sea salt
- ¼ teaspoon freshly ground black pepper
- 1 cup (240 mL) safflower oil or other frying oil

1. In a large skillet, heat the avocado oil over medium-high heat. Add the cauliflower and cook for about 10 minutes, stirring frequently, until the florets are golden brown.

2. Put the onion and garlic in a food processor. Pulse about five times, until the onion is chopped but still chunky. Add the browned cauliflower to the food processor and pulse another five times, until the cauliflower is chopped and chunky.

3. Add the arrowroot flour, almond flour, parsley, coriander, cumin, egg, salt, and pepper to the food processor. Pulse about ten times, until well combined. Use a rubber spatula to scrape down the sides and pulse a few more times if necessary. The mixture should be chunky but well combined.

4. In a deep skillet, heat the safflower oil over medium-high heat. Line a large plate with paper towels. Once the oil begins to bubble and spit, use a small ice cream scoop to scoop about 2 tablespoons of the batter and gently drop it into the oil. You want to tightly pack the batter into the scoop so it stays together once you place it in the oil. Fry about 6 falafel at a time to avoid crowding.

5. After about 3 minutes, the edges will look golden brown. Use tongs to flip the falafel, then cook for another couple of minutes until they are browned and

crispy. Transfer to the paper towel–lined plate and continue frying until all the batter is used. (The oil in the skillet should be enough to fry all the falafel.)

6. Falafel can be stored in an airtight container in the fridge for about 1 week. Reheat under the broiler for 1 to 2 minutes to regain crispiness.

Note: Arrowroot flour is also known as arrowroot starch or arrowroot powder.

BLT

WITH CAULIFLOWER MAYO

....

BLTS ARE A summertime staple. When you have perfectly ripe tomatoes, there is nothing better. There are so many ways to customize them too: add some avocado or, if you're vegetarian, swap the bacon for smoked tempeh. And as much as I love a classic mayonnaise—for spreading, slathering, and dipping—I also love options (especially healthier ones). You can spice up this cauliflower mayo by replacing the lemon juice with lime and adding a teaspoon of chipotle chile powder to make a condiment with a kick.

SERVES 4, WITH EXTRA MAYO TO SPARE

....

FOR THE CAULIFLOWER MAYONNAISE

- 1 cup (105 g) cauliflower rice (see page 18)
- 1 large egg
- ¼ cup (60 mL) avocado oil
- Juice of 1 lemon
- 1 tablespoon cider vinegar
- 1 tablespoon Dijon mustard
- ⅛ teaspoon sea salt

FOR THE SANDWICH

- 8 slices sourdough, Seeded Sandwich Bread (page 96), or your favorite sandwich bread
- 4 slices bacon, cooked
- 4 leaves of green leaf lettuce
- 1 ripe tomato, sliced
- 1 ripe avocado, sliced

1. Bring an inch of water to a boil in a small saucepan. Place the cauliflower rice in a steamer basket set over the boiling water. Cover and steam for 5 minutes, until the rice is softened and translucent around the edges.

2. Place the steamed cauliflower rice, egg, avocado oil, lemon juice, vinegar, mustard, and salt in a high-powered blender. Blend until the ingredients are completely combined. Use a rubber spatula to scrape down the sides and blend again until smooth and creamy. Transfer to an airtight container and chill for at least 2 hours. The mayo will keep for a couple of weeks in the fridge.

3. To assemble the sandwiches, toast the bread. Spread the mayo on both sides of the toast. Layer the bacon, lettuce, tomato, and avocado slices on 4 slices of toast. Top each with the remaining bread and serve.

SEEDED SANDWICH BREAD

TURNS OUT THE trick to making moist homemade sandwich bread is cauliflower rice. This recipe yields a loaf that's easy to slice, store, and toast. Use it to make a gooey grilled cheese sandwich, or double-toast a thin slice (making it crunchy on the outside but still soft and fluffy on the inside) and serve it with whipped cream cheese and strawberry jam.

MAKES ONE 9 BY 5-INCH (23 BY 13 CM) LOAF; SERVES 10

- 3 cups (315 g) cauliflower rice (see page 18)
- 6 large eggs
- ½ cup (112 g) tahini
- 1 cup (115 g) blanched almond flour (see Note, page 31)
- ½ cup (68 g) tapioca flour
- ¼ cup (27 g) ground flax meal
- 1 teaspoon baking powder
- 1 teaspoon baking soda
- 1 teaspoon sea salt
- 2 tablespoons cider vinegar
- 1 tablespoon whole flax seeds
- 1 tablespoon sesame seeds
- 1 tablespoon sunflower seeds

1. Preheat the oven to 350°F (180°C). Line the bottom of a 9 by 5-inch (23 by 13 cm) bread pan with parchment paper.

2. Place the cauliflower rice in a dry sauté pan over medium-high heat. Stir frequently for about 5 minutes, until it softens and looks translucent.

3. Once cooled to the touch, transfer the rice to the center of a clean, thin dish towel. Working over the sink, gather the corners and squeeze out the excess liquid. Set aside.

4. Place the eggs and tahini in a high-powered blender and blend on high until well combined and bubbly, about 30 seconds. Add the cauliflower rice and blend until smooth, about 1 minute.

5. Add the almond flour, tapioca flour, flax meal, baking powder, baking soda, and salt to the blender. Blend until completely combined and smooth, about 1 minute.

6. Add the vinegar to the blender and blend for about 10 seconds. Let the mixture stand for 5 minutes.

7. Pour the batter into the prepared pan. Sprinkle the top of the bread with the whole flax seeds, sesame seeds, and sunflower seeds. Bake for 1 hour.

8. Allow the bread to come to room temperature before cutting into it. Store it in the fridge for up to a week, or slice and store tightly wrapped in the freezer for up to 3 months.

SWEET POTATO NOODLES
WITH CAULIFLOWER CARBONARA SAUCE

SPIRALIZING HAS BECOME my favorite way to prepare sweet potatoes as it makes for a great-tasting stand-in for traditional noodles. I use a spiralizer that clamps onto my kitchen counter and lets me turn veggies (and some fruit) into different-shaped noodles by turning a crank. Nowadays you can find prespiralized veggies in most local grocery stores (often near the premade salads). Aside from the fun, twirly shape and added flavor that spiralized sweet potatoes lend to a dish, they can be ready to eat in under 10 minutes. Simply cook them in oil for a few minutes, tossing with tongs, then add a tablespoon of water to help steam and soften the noodles. Top them with this lightened carbonara sauce or play around with different sauces like Kale Pesto (page 79), Cilantro-Lime Pesto (page 80), or Sweet Basil Marinara Sauce (page 113).

SERVES 4

- 1 cup (105 g) cauliflower rice (see page 18)
- 1 cup (240 mL) whole milk
- 1 cup (120 g) shredded Gruyère
- 2 garlic cloves
- ½ teaspoon sea salt
- 1 tablespoon avocado oil
- 1 large sweet potato (about 32 ounces/907 g), spiralized into noodles
- 1 cup (113 g) cubed pancetta
- ¼ cup (9 g) chopped fresh sage leaves
- ¼ cup (30 g) shaved Parmesan

1. Bring an inch of water to a boil in a small saucepan. Place the cauliflower rice in a steamer basket set over the boiling water. Cover and steam for 5 minutes, until the rice is softened and translucent around the edges.

2. Transfer the steamed cauliflower to a high-powered blender along with the milk, Gruyère, garlic, and salt. Blend the sauce until smooth, about 1 minute.

3. Pour the sauce into a saucepan over medium-high heat and bring to a boil. Reduce the heat to medium and continue to simmer, whisking frequently, for 5 to 10 minutes, until the sauce thickens.

4. Heat the avocado oil in a large skillet over medium-high heat. Add the sweet potato noodles and cook for 3 minutes, using tongs to toss frequently. After 3 minutes, add 1 tablespoon water, the pancetta, and most of the sage, reserving some to top the pasta. The water will steam the noodles, leaving them with a soft but al dente texture.

5. Cook for another 2 to 3 minutes, tossing frequently, until the water has evaporated and the noodles are bright orange and just tender.

6. Reduce the heat to low and add the sauce to the pan. Use tongs to toss and fully coat the noodles, then remove from the heat.

7. Plate the noodles. Top with the remaining sage and some shaved Parmesan before serving.

HAPPY HOUR

CAULIFLOWER CAN LIGHTEN up foods that you might otherwise try to avoid. Love queso dip? Making a dairy-free cauliflower queso takes it from a heavy appetizer to a lighter, nutrient-dense version without skimping on the flavor! Nachos, Buffalo wings, and even rice balls can be transformed when you make them with cauliflower. What better way to kick off an evening of drinks and dining than with giving your guests some foods that won't weigh them down or fill them up. Serve these dishes for game-day eats or as appetizers for your next party. They're guaranteed to keep all your guests happy, whether they're vegetarian, vegan, gluten-free, or even omnivorous.

· ✳ ·

VEGAN QUESO

LET'S BE REAL: Cheese makes everything taste better. But there are lots of reasons we might not want to consume dairy. And when that's the case, this thick and cheesy vegan queso will come to the rescue. Cheese is replaced with nutritional yeast, a deactivated yeast that has a cheesy taste. It's a significant source of B-complex vitamins and has trace amounts of other vitamins and minerals. Use vegan queso in place of cheese in everything from mac and cheese to pesto, or serve it on top of Skillet Nachos (page 114) and tacos.

MAKES 5 CUPS; SERVES 10

- 1½ cups (200 g) cauliflower florets (page 16)
- 1 cup (262 g) store-bought medium salsa
- ½ cup (71 g) raw cashews
- ⅓ cup (27 g) nutritional yeast
- 2 garlic cloves
- 2 teaspoons ground cumin
- ½ teaspoon sea salt
- Coarsely chopped cilantro, for garnish
- Tortilla chips, sliced bell pepper, or carrots, for serving (optional)

1. Bring an inch of water to a boil in a medium saucepan. Place the cauliflower in a steamer basket set over the boiling water. Cover and steam for about 5 minutes, until the florets are easily pierced with a fork.

2. Combine the cooked cauliflower, salsa, cashews, nutritional yeast, garlic, cumin, and salt in a high-powered blender. Blend on high until smooth and creamy, about 1 minute.

3. Use a rubber spatula to scrape down the sides and blend for another 10 seconds to puree the queso.

4. Enjoy the dip warm and garnished with chopped cilantro. Serve the dip with your favorite tortilla chips or sliced veggies like bell pepper or carrots. Leftovers can be kept in an airtight container in the fridge for up to 1 week. Reheat on the stovetop, whisking in some unsweetened almond milk if the queso gets too thick.

CARAMELIZED ONION CAULIFLOWER HUMMUS

ADDING CAULIFLOWER TO hummus will boost the nutrients as well as the flavor. Serve the dip with rainbow carrot sticks, sugar snap peas, or your favorite pita crackers. It's delicious as is, but you can play around with adding different flavors to the mix: garlic and sun-dried tomato are two of the tastiest variations (see opposite).

MAKES 4 CUPS

- 4 cups (540 g) small cauliflower florets (see page 16)
- 1 onion, chopped
- 6 tablespoons (90 mL) avocado oil
- 7 garlic cloves
- ½ cup (83 g) canned chickpeas, drained and rinsed
- Juice of ½ lemon
- 1 teaspoon sea salt
- ¼ teaspoon freshly ground black pepper
- 1 tablespoon extra-virgin olive oil, for drizzling
- ¼ cup (31 g) pine nuts, toasted, for topping
- Rainbow carrots, snap peas, and/or pita chips, for dipping

1. Place the cauliflower florets, onion, 2 tablespoons of the avocado oil, and 2 of the garlic cloves in a large skillet set over medium-high heat. Cook for 15 to 20 minutes, stirring frequently, until the vegetables are golden brown.

2. Transfer the cauliflower mixture to a food processor. Add the chickpeas, lemon juice, 3 tablespoons of the avocado oil, ¼ cup (60 mL) water, salt, and pepper. Process for about 5 minutes, taking breaks to scrape down the sides with a rubber spatula.

3. While the hummus is processing, place the remaining 5 garlic cloves in a small skillet with the remaining 1 tablespoon avocado oil. Cook, stirring frequently, over medium-low heat for about 10 minutes to caramelize the garlic cloves.

4. Transfer the cauliflower hummus to a bowl and drizzle with your favorite olive oil, if desired.

5. Top with the sautéed garlic cloves, sprinkle with pine nuts if you wish, and serve with the dippers of your choice.

6. Hummus will keep for up to 1 week in an airtight container in the fridge. Have leftovers? Wrap up some veggies and hummus in a collard green leaf or spread some hummus on a roasted eggplant and pepper sandwich.

VARIATIONS

Turn this recipe into garlic hummus by adding 7 more
cloves when blending the hummus. Or make a sun-dried
tomato hummus by adding 1 cup sun-dried tomatoes
when you process the other ingredients.

BUFFALO JACKFRUIT DIP

JACKFRUIT IS A tropical fruit that makes an excellent meat substitute. While you can often find the fresh fruit in the produce section of your grocery store, you can buy it canned too. It's important to look for canned jackfruit that is packed in water because brines and other canning liquids will give it a funky taste that you want to avoid. Once jackfruit is sautéed and softened, it pulls apart very much like shredded chicken or pulled pork and really takes on the flavors that surround it, as in this cheesy buffalo dip. You can make your own Wing Sauce and Ranch Dressing or use store-bought if you're short on time.

SERVES 6 TO 8

- 5 cups (675 g) cauliflower florets (see page 16)
- 8 ounces (227 g) cream cheese
- 1 cup (242 g) homemade Wing Sauce (recipe follows) or store-bought
- ½ cup (123 g) homemade Ranch Dressing (recipe follows) or store-bought
- 2 garlic cloves
- 1¼ cups (150 g) shredded Cheddar
- 3 17-ounce (482 g) cans water-packed jackfruit, drained and rinsed
- 2 tablespoons avocado oil
- Chopped fresh parsley, for garnish
- Crackers or celery sticks, for serving

1. Preheat the oven to 350°F (180°C).

2. Bring an inch of water to a boil in a large saucepan. Place the cauliflower in a steamer basket set over the boiling water. Cover and steam for about 5 minutes, until the florets are easily pierced with a fork.

3. In a high-powered blender, combine the steamed cauliflower, cream cheese, Wing Sauce, Ranch Dressing, garlic cloves, and 1 cup (120 g) of the Cheddar. Blend on high until smooth and creamy. Use a rubber spatula to scrape down the sides and blend for another 10 seconds until fully combined. Set aside.

4. Place the jackfruit on a cutting board. Sort through the pieces, looking for the hard triangular center core. Cut that part away and discard.

5. Heat the avocado oil in a large skillet over medium-high heat. Add the jackfruit to the hot oil. After about 3 minutes, use a spatula to break up the jackfruit pieces and pull them apart. The texture should start to resemble pulled pork or shredded chicken.

6. Continue to stir and break apart the jackfruit for about 8 minutes, until it softens, appears shredded, and begins to turn golden brown.

CONTINUED

7. Pour half of the Wing Sauce into a baking dish. Add the jackfruit and cover with the rest of the sauce. Top with the remaining shredded Cheddar and bake for 15 minutes, until bubbly and heated through.

8. Garnish with fresh parsley and serve with your favorite crackers, celery sticks, or other sliced vegetables. Leftover dip can be stored in an airtight container in the fridge for up to 1 week.

WING SAUCE

MAKES 1 CUP (242 G/245 ML)

- 8 tablespoons (1 stick/113 g) unsalted butter or ½ cup (120 g) ghee
- ½ cup (120 mL) hot sauce
- 1½ tablespoons white vinegar
- ¼ teaspoon Worcestershire sauce
- ¼ teaspoon cayenne pepper
- ¼ teaspoon freshly ground black pepper
- ¼ teaspoon garlic powder

In a small saucepan over medium-high heat, melt the butter and whisk in the hot sauce until combined. Add the vinegar, Worcestershire, cayenne, black pepper, and garlic powder. Whisk together and bring to a simmer, then remove from the heat and allow to cool to room temperature. Store in the fridge for about one week and reheat as needed.

RANCH DRESSING

MAKES ABOUT 1 CUP (246 G/215 ML)

- ½ cup (108 g) mayonnaise (use avocado oil mayonnaise, if you prefer)
- ¼ cup (60 mL) heavy cream (regular milk or unsweetened canned coconut cream also works)
- ½ teaspoon dried dill
- ½ teaspoon garlic powder
- ½ teaspoon onion powder
- ¼ teaspoon sea salt
- ¼ teaspoon freshly ground black pepper

Whisk together the mayonnaise, cream, dill, garlic powder, onion powder, salt, and pepper in a medium bowl. Once smooth, transfer to a lidded jar and store in the fridge for up to 10 days.

CHEESY CAULIFLOWER RICE BALLS

WITH SWEET BASIL MARINARA SAUCE

....

THE KEY TO making these rice balls is tucking the cheese into the center of the cauliflower rice and squeezing the rice tightly around it. You need to make the balls compact so they'll hold together when fried. Make an easy homemade marinara to use as your dipping sauce.

MAKES 6 TO 8 BALLS;
SERVES 2 TO 4 PEOPLE

- 2 cups (270 g) cauliflower rice (see page 18)
- 2 large eggs
- 1 teaspoon garlic powder
- 1 teaspoon onion powder
- ½ teaspoon dried oregano
- ½ teaspoon sea salt
- ⅓ cup (40 g) shredded Parmesan
- ½ cup (57 g) blanched almond flour (see Note, page 31)
- ¼ cup (32 g) mozzarella cubes
- 2 cups (480 mL) safflower oil, for frying
- 1 cup Sweet Basil Marinara Sauce, for serving (recipe follows)

1. Place the cauliflower rice in a microwave-safe bowl with 1 tablespoon water. Cover the bowl loosely with a paper towel and microwave for 4 minutes, until tender. If you don't have a microwave, cook the rice in a large skillet for about 3 minutes, stirring frequently. Add 1 tablespoon water and continue to cook for another 3 minutes, until the water has evaporated and the rice has softened. Press a paper towel or clean, thin dish towel onto the rice to absorb excess moisture and place the rice in a medium bowl.

2. Add 1 egg along with the garlic powder, onion powder, oregano, salt, and Parmesan to the cauliflower. Fold to combine thoroughly.

3. In a small shallow bowl, whisk the remaining egg. Put the almond flour in another small bowl. These will be your "stations" for coating the rice balls.

4. Pinch off a golf ball–size piece of the rice mixture. Insert a mozzarella cube into the center and squeeze the mixture in your hand until it forms a ball again with the cheese entirely enclosed inside.

5. Toss the rice ball in the almond flour until coated. These are super forgiving, so if the ball falls apart, just re-form it with your hands. Next dip it in the beaten egg, then roll it in the almond flour again until coated.

CONTINUED ....

6. Set aside on a plate and continue with the rest of the cauliflower rice mixture.

7. Heat the safflower oil in a medium frying pan over high heat for 4 minutes. Reduce the heat to medium-high and place about 4 balls in the oil. When the bottoms of the balls are golden brown, about 2 minutes, flip the balls and fry the other side for 2 minutes.

8. Transfer to a paper towel–lined plate and cook the second batch of rice balls. Transfer to a serving plate and serve with marinara sauce.

SWEET BASIL MARINARA SAUCE

MAKES ABOUT 4 CUPS

- 1 28-ounce (794 g) can fire-roasted crushed tomatoes
- 3 tablespoons finely chopped fresh basil
- 2 tablespoons coconut sugar (honey, maple syrup, or agave nectar also work; see Note, page 25)
- 3 garlic cloves, minced
- 1 teaspoon dried oregano
- 1 teaspoon onion powder
- ¼ teaspoon sea salt
- ¼ teaspoon freshly ground black pepper

1. Combine the tomatoes, basil, coconut sugar, garlic, oregano, onion powder, salt, and pepper in a medium saucepan over medium-high heat. Bring the sauce to a low boil, stirring frequently.

2. Reduce the heat to medium-low and simmer for 5 to 10 minutes. If not using immediately, let cool to room temperature, then transfer to an airtight container and store in the fridge for up to 10 days.

1. Place a mozzarella cube in the center of a golf ball–size mound of cauliflower rice.

2. Squeeze the mixture in your hand until it forms a ball. The cheese cube should be completely enclosed.

3. Coat the rice ball in the almond flour. Reform the ball with your hands (if needed), dip the ball in the egg, and then once again in the almond flour.

4. When the rice balls are fried until crispy and golden brown on the outside, they'll be melted on the inside.

SKILLET NACHOS

LIGHTEN UP YOUR nacho habit with the help of cauliflower. Nutritious florets stand in for traditional tortilla chips, but all your favorite nacho flavors still show up to party. I have pretty high standards when it comes to cheesy, loaded nachos, and I promise this fresh take on your favorite game-day appetizer does not disappoint. If you're vegan, skip the Cheddar and top with Vegan Queso (page 103) instead.

SERVES 4

- 5 cups (675 g) cauliflower florets (see page 16)
- 3 tablespoons avocado oil
- ¼ cup (28 g) homemade Taco Seasoning (recipe follows) or store-bought
- 1 ear of corn
- 1 cup (120 g) shredded Cheddar
- 6 tablespoons (90 mL) salsa
- ¼ cup (60 g) canned black beans, drained and rinsed
- ¼ red onion, finely chopped
- 1 avocado, sliced
- ¼ cup (10 g) fresh cilantro leaves, for garnish

1. Preheat the oven to 400°F (200°C).

2. In a large bowl, toss the florets with the avocado oil until coated. Add the Taco Seasoning and toss again to evenly coat. Transfer the florets to an ovenproof skillet and spread them out in a single layer across the bottom. Roast for about 30 minutes, until the edges are browned and crispy.

3. While the cauliflower is roasting, bring a medium pot of water to a boil. Boil the corn for 5 minutes. Drain, let cool, and cut the kernels off the cob. Set aside.

4. When the cauliflower is tender, remove the skillet from the oven and sprinkle the Cheddar over the florets. Return the skillet to the oven for another 2 minutes, until the cheese is melted.

5. To finish the nachos, drop tablespoons of salsa randomly on top of the cauliflower and scatter the black beans, corn kernels, and red onion over all. Top with the sliced avocado and cilantro.

6. To serve, scoop some skillet nachos with a large spoon onto individual plates for eating with a fork, or bring the entire skillet to the table and provide toothpicks for spearing the florets.

TACO SEASONING

MAKES ABOUT ¼ CUP (28 G)

- 1 tablespoon chili powder
- 1½ teaspoons ground cumin
- 1 teaspoon sea salt
- ½ teaspoon paprika
- ¼ teaspoon garlic powder
- ¼ teaspoon onion powder
- ¼ teaspoon dried oregano
- ¼ teaspoon red pepper flakes

In a small bowl, mix together the chili powder, cumin, salt, paprika, garlic powder, onion powder, oregano, and red pepper flakes. The mixture will keep in an airtight container for up to 1 month in your pantry.

BUFFALO CAULIFLOWER WINGS

YOU CAN REPLICATE Buffalo wings by substituting fried cauliflower. The florets get soft on the inside but stay crisp on the outside, and are flavored with spicy wing sauce. This recipe uses a mix of tapioca and almond flours to give the cauliflower a light, gluten-free breading, but you could use all-purpose flour if gluten is not an issue.

SERVES 4

- 5 cups (675 g) cauliflower florets (see page 16)
- ½ cup (68 g) tapioca flour
- ½ cup (57 g) blanched almond flour (see Note, page 31)
- 1 teaspoon dry mustard
- 1 teaspoon smoked paprika
- 1 teaspoon garlic powder
- 2 cups (480 mL) safflower oil, or your favorite frying oil
- 1 cup (242 g) Wing Sauce (page 109)
- 3 celery stalks, cut into 3-inch (8 cm) pieces
- ½ cup (123 g) Ranch Dressing (page 109)

1. Bring an inch of water to a boil in a medium saucepan. Place the cauliflower in a steamer basket set over the boiling water. Cover and steam for about 5 minutes, until the florets are tender.

2. Make the breading: In a medium bowl, whisk together the tapioca flour, almond flour, dry mustard, smoked paprika, and garlic powder.

3. When the florets are tender, drop a handful into the breading and coat generously (you don't need to pat them dry after steaming). Transfer the breaded florets to a clean plate.

4. Heat the oil in a large frying pan over high heat. Once your thermometer reads between 325°F and 375°F (165°C and 190°C), or when bubbles appear around the handle of a wooden spoon when you dip it into the oil, reduce the heat to medium-high. Add the breaded florets to the pan, one at a time, about 2 inches (5 cm) apart. Don't crowd them; you'll need to do this in two or three batches to fry all the florets.

5. After 3 minutes, once the edges of the florets turn golden brown, use tongs to flip the cauliflower and cook for another 2 minutes. Transfer to a paper towel–lined plate and continue until all the florets have been fried.

6. Transfer to a serving dish and drizzle with the Wing Sauce. Serve with celery stalks and Ranch Dressing for dipping.

COCONUT-CRUSTED CAULIFLOWER POPPERS

WITH MINT PESTO

IF YOU LIKE coconut-crusted shrimp, you will love these coconut cauliflower poppers. The unsweetened shredded coconut gives them a sweet, crispy crunch. They're good on their own, but you can serve them with a sweet mint pesto for a great flavor combination.

SERVES 6 TO 8

FOR THE POPPERS

- 3 cups (405 g) medium cauliflower florets (see page 16)
- 2 large eggs
- 1 cup (85 g) unsweetened shredded coconut
- ½ cup (60 g) grated Parmesan
- 1 teaspoon sea salt
- 1 teaspoon garlic powder
- 2 cups (480 mL) safflower oil

FOR THE MINT PESTO

- 1 cup (125 g) pine nuts
- 1 cup (40 g) fresh mint leaves
- ½ cup (10 g) fresh basil leaves
- ¼ cup (60 mL) avocado oil
- 1 tablespoon agave nectar (see Note, page 25)
- 2 garlic cloves
- ½ teaspoon sea salt

1. Bring an inch of water to a boil in a medium saucepan. Place the cauliflower in a steamer basket set over the boiling water. Cover and steam for about 5 minutes, until the florets are tender but still firm.

2. While the cauliflower is cooking, whisk both eggs in a shallow bowl. In a separate bowl, mix the shredded coconut, Parmesan cheese, sea salt, and garlic powder. Set a large plate next to the bowls.

3. Set the steamed florets aside on a plate or on a clean dish towel until cool enough to handle. With one hand, dip a floret into the coconut mixture until coated. Then drop the coated floret into the beaten egg and use your other hand to turn it over until it's well coated. Hold it over the bowl to allow any excess egg to drip off. Drop it back in the bowl with the coconut mixture and use your other (coconut) hand to coat the floret with the coconut mixture again. Place the coated florets on a large plate. Continue this process until all the florets are coated.

4. Line a large plate with paper towels and set it near the stove. Pour the oil into a stockpot until it comes about 2 inches (5 cm) up the side. Heat the oil over high heat for about 4 minutes, until it's almost bubbling and your thermometer reads between 325°F and 375°F (165°C and 190°C), or when bubbles appear

around the handle of a wooden spoon when you dip it into the oil. Working in batches, gently drop 8 to 10 florets into the oil and fry for about 3 minutes, until the outside is crispy and golden brown. Use a slotted spoon to remove the poppers and allow the excess oil to drip away. Transfer to the paper towel–lined plate. Continue to fry the florets in batches until all are cooked.

5. Meanwhile, make the pesto: Place the pine nuts, mint, basil, avocado oil, agave nectar, garlic, and salt in a food processor and process for 20 seconds. Use a rubber spatula to scrape down the sides, then process for another 20 seconds. Transfer to a small bowl.

6. Transfer the poppers to a serving dish and enjoy with the mint pesto for dipping.

NACHO CAULI TOSTADAS

YOU CAN TOP these little tostadas with whatever you're craving. Add some fresh avocado, some shredded barbecued chicken, or a dollop of salsa for a tasty appetizer. Not in the mood for Southwest flavors? Ditch the pepper Jack and Taco Seasoning and substitute Gruyère and chopped rosemary.

**MAKES 24 TOSTADAS;
SERVES 6**

- 4 cups (540 g) medium cauliflower florets (see page 16)
- 1½ cups (180 g) cubed pepper Jack cheese
- 3 tablespoons Taco Seasoning (page 115)
- ¼ cup (10 g) chopped fresh cilantro leaves
- ½ cup Vegan Queso (page 103) or salsa
- 1 avocado, cut into cubes

1. Preheat the oven to 400°F (200°C). Line 2 baking sheets with parchment paper. Set one oven rack in the middle and one beneath the broiler.

2. Using the chopping blade on your food processor, process a handful of florets at a time for about 30 seconds, until completely chopped into the consistency of meal (see page 19). Transfer the meal to a clean, thin dish towel or piece of cheesecloth and continue this process until all the florets are chopped. Do this in two or three batches; if you put all the florets in the food processor at once, they won't get evenly grated.

3. Once all the meal is in the dish towel, gather the corners and, working over the sink, squeeze out as much liquid as you can. Put the squeezed cauliflower in a large bowl.

4. Quickly rinse out the food processor (it doesn't have to be perfectly clean) and add the cubed cheese. Process for about 20 seconds, until chopped.

5. Add the chopped cheese to the bowl of cauliflower meal along with the Taco Seasoning and cilantro (save a little to use as a garnish). Use a rubber spatula to mix everything together.

6. Work in batches to bake the tostadas. Use a small ice cream scoop (or a tablespoon) to make eight 2-inch (5 cm) balls of the cauliflower mixture and place them on the prepared baking sheets, about 2 inches (5 cm)

apart. Use a spatula to flatten the balls. Use your fingers to re-form the flattened balls into circles as needed.

7. Bake for 18 to 20 minutes, then broil on high for 2 minutes, until golden brown. Remove from the oven and cook the second batch. Allow each batch to cool on the baking sheet for 5 minutes, then transfer to a cooling rack. Use the first baking sheet for the third batch of tostadas and repeat until all three batches are baked.

8. Top the tostadas with some queso or salsa, avocado, and more cilantro for garnish. Tostadas are best eaten immediately.

4

DINNER

YOU PROBABLY ALREADY eat cauliflower for dinner often. But there are so many unexpected ways you can incorporate cauliflower into your evening meal. This chapter pushes those ideas forward and will have you thinking outside the roasted cauliflower floret. Use cauliflower as a rice base for a poke bowl, to coat chicken with a "breading," or to create a vegetarian taco filling. You can even treat cauliflower like a meat lover's steak and serve it over some parsnip mash with gravy.

.... ✳ ....

TUNA POKE BOWLS
WITH CAULIFLOWER RICE

POKE BOWLS, THE beloved Hawaiian dish of fish, rice, and toppings that can be anything from crispy onions to pineapple to edamame, are wildly popular because the food is both fresh and good for you. Make healthier poke bowls at home using cauliflower rice as the base.

SERVES 2

FOR THE TUNA POKE

- 1 pound (454 g) sushi-grade tuna
- 3 tablespoons soy sauce
- 1 tablespoon seasoned rice vinegar
- 1 teaspoon toasted sesame oil
- 2 garlic cloves, minced
- 1 teaspoon grated fresh ginger
- 1 scallion, light green part only, thinly sliced
- 1 teaspoon black sesame seeds

FOR THE BOWL

- 1 tablespoon avocado oil
- 3 cups (315 g) cauliflower rice (see page 18)
- 1 tablespoon seasoned rice vinegar
- 1 teaspoon toasted sesame oil
- Sea salt
- 1 cup (118 g) frozen shelled edamame
- 1 avocado, sliced
- 1 small cucumber, diced
- 2 teaspoons sesame seeds
- 1 scallion, light green part only, thinly sliced

1. Use a sharp butcher's knife to cut the tuna into ½-inch (1 cm) to 1-inch (3 cm) cubes.

2. In a large bowl, mix the tuna, soy sauce, rice vinegar, sesame oil, garlic, ginger, scallion, and sesame seeds. Refrigerate for 10 minutes so the tuna can absorb the flavors.

3. For the rice bowl, heat the avocado oil in a large skillet over medium-high heat. When the oil starts to sizzle, add the cauliflower rice to the pan. Cook for about 3 minutes, until the rice begins to soften and the edges appear translucent. Add the rice vinegar, sesame oil, and salt to taste. Continue to cook for another 3 minutes, until the rice is heated through.

4. Simmer the shelled edamame in water for 5 minutes, or microwave on high for about 3 minutes, stirring every minute.

5. Divide the cauliflower rice between 2 bowls. Top each bowl with some poke, avocado, cucumber, and edamame. Sprinkle sesame seeds and scallions over the top.

TURMERIC ROASTED VEGETABLE BUDDHA BOWL

....

ON NIGHTS WHEN you can't wrap your head around making a full dinner, roast a bunch of veggies, put them in a bowl with a delicious dressing, and call it a Buddha bowl. Add a special rice to the mix, like Turmeric Cauliflower Rice (page 174) or Garlic-Parmesan Cauliflower Rice (page 173). The tahini dressing ties the ingredients together into one savory and satisfying dinner.

SERVES 4

FOR THE ROASTED VEGGIES

- 6 cups (810 g) cauliflower florets (see page 16)
- 6 cups (680 g) Brussels sprouts, ends trimmed, cut in half lengthwise
- 2 tablespoons avocado oil
- 2 teaspoons turmeric
- ½ teaspoon smoked paprika
- ½ teaspoon sea salt
- ¼ teaspoon freshly ground black pepper

FOR THE TAHINI DRESSING

- ½ cup (120 g) tahini
- 3 garlic cloves, minced
- 2 tablespoons refined coconut oil, melted
- 1 tablespoon coconut nectar, honey, agave nectar or maple syrup (see Note, page 25)
- ⅛ teaspoon sea salt

(continued)

1. Preheat the oven to 400°F (200°C). Line a baking sheet with parchment paper.

2. Place the cauliflower and Brussels sprouts in a large bowl. Toss with the avocado oil. Add the turmeric, paprika, salt, and pepper and toss again. Place on the prepared baking sheet and roast for 40 to 50 minutes, until tender and brown. If the veggies need a little help crisping up, place them under the broiler for a few minutes.

3. While the veggies are roasting, make the dressing: In a small bowl, whisk together the tahini, garlic, coconut oil, coconut nectar, and salt.

4. Divide the arugula, cabbage, and chickpeas among 4 serving bowls. When the veggies are roasted, add those. Place a dollop of hummus (recipe follows) in each bowl and drizzle with the tahini dressing. Serve with rice, if desired.

- 5½ cups (113 g) arugula

- 2 cups red cabbage, shredded

- 1 15-ounce (425 g) can chickpeas, drained and rinsed

- ½ cup (120 mL) Hummus (recipe follows)

- Rice, or cauliflower rice (see page 18) for serving (optional)

HUMMUS

MAKES 2 CUPS (240 ML)

- 1 15-ounce (425 g) can chickpeas, drained and rinsed

- ¼ cup (60 mL) extra-virgin olive oil

- ¼ cup (60 mL) lemon juice (from 2 lemons)

- 2 garlic cloves

- 1 teaspoon ground cumin

- ½ teaspoon chipotle chile powder

- ½ teaspoon sea salt

1. Put the chickpeas, olive oil, lemon juice, garlic, cumin, chipotle chile powder, and salt in a food processor. Process for about 30 seconds. Use a rubber spatula to scrape down the sides and process again until thoroughly combined. Add 1 tablespoon water at a time, blending after each addition, until the hummus is smooth.

2. Store hummus in an airtight container in the fridge for up to 1 week.

CAULIFLOWER CARROT FRITTERS

WITH SPICY CASHEW AÏOLI

ON NIGHTS WHEN you're eating meatless, fritters are a good way to get a lot of veggies into your diet without skimping on flavor. Serve these fritters on top of a salad, in a veggie wrap, or piled onto your plate for a hearty vegetarian meal. The cashews give the aïoli a creamy consistency while keeping it dairy-free.

MAKES 12 FRITTERS

FOR THE SPICY CASHEW AÏOLI

- 1 cup (142 g) raw cashews
- Juice of 1 lemon
- 2 garlic cloves
- 2 tablespoons avocado oil
- ½ teaspoon chipotle chile powder
- ¼ teaspoon smoked paprika
- ¼ teaspoon sea salt

FOR THE FRITTERS

- 4 cups (420 g) cauliflower rice (see page 18)
- 1 sweet onion, finely chopped
- 1 carrot, shredded
- 2 large eggs
- 3 garlic cloves, minced
- 2 tablespoons chopped fresh chives, plus more for garnish
- ¼ cup (170 g) arrowroot flour
- ½ teaspoon sea salt
- ¼ cup (60 mL) refined coconut oil, for frying

1. Make the aïoli: Combine the cashews and 1 cup (240 mL) room-temperature water in a bowl so the water covers the cashews. Soak the cashews for at least 2 hours, or refrigerate them and soak overnight. Alternatively, you could boil the cashews for 10 minutes to soften them.

2. Drain the nuts, discarding the soaking water, and place in a food processor or blender along with 2 tablespoons water, the lemon juice, garlic, avocado oil, chipotle chile powder, paprika, and salt. Process until smooth, about 2 minutes, taking breaks every 30 seconds to scrape down the sides of the food processor with a rubber spatula. Set aside.

3. Make the fritters: Place the cauliflower rice, onion, carrot, eggs, garlic, and chives in a large bowl. Fold to combine. Sprinkle with the arrowroot flour and salt. Fold again until the dry ingredients are well incorporated and then set aside for 5 minutes to rest.

4. Heat the oven to 300°F (150°C). Line a baking sheet with parchment paper and set aside.

5. Prep the fritters: Use a small ice cream scoop or a tablespoon to scoop a 2- to 3-inch (5 to 8 cm) ball of the cauliflower mixture into your hand. Firmly

squeeze the ball in your palm to make it compact and press out any excess liquid. Place the balls on a clean plate.

6. In a large skillet, warm 2 tablespoons of the coconut oil over high heat. When the oil starts to simmer, reduce the heat to medium-high. Place 3 to 4 balls in the oil and fry for about 1 minute.

7. Use the back of a spatula to gently press down and flatten the fritters. Fry for another 2 to 3 minutes, until the edges turn golden brown. Gently flip the fritters and fry the other side for 2 to 3 minutes, until golden brown. Transfer to the prepared baking sheet and place in the oven to keep warm.

8. Continue working in batches, 2 or 3 fritters at a time, until the cauliflower mixture is used up. Add extra coconut oil to the pan, as needed, between batches. Discard any excess liquid left behind in the bowl.

9. Top each fritter with the spicy aïoli and extra chives and enjoy. The fritters and aïoli should be stored separately. Place parchment paper between each fritter and store in an airtight container in the fridge for up to 5 days. Fritters are best reheated in the microwave or in the oven at a low temperature (about 300°F/150°C) until warm. Leftover aïoli can be stored in an airtight container in the fridge for up to 1 week.

THAI CURRY MEATBALLS

ONCE YOU TRY these chicken-cauliflower meatballs, you'll find every excuse to make them again. Prep them on a Sunday to serve with a spaghetti dinner. The next night, eat them with some roasted veggies. Leftovers make a great work lunch. You can even arrange them on your best platter and serve them as hors d'oeuvres at your next party.

MAKES 24 MEATBALLS

FOR THE MEATBALLS

- 1 pound (454 g) ground chicken
- 1 cup (105 g) cauliflower rice (see page 18)
- ¼ sweet onion, finely chopped
- ¼ cup (30 g) blanched almond flour (see Note)
- 2 tablespoons chopped fresh cilantro leaves, plus more for garnish (optional)
- 1 teaspoon toasted sesame oil
- 1 teaspoon grated fresh ginger
- 2 garlic cloves, minced
- 2 large eggs
- 1 tablespoon soy sauce
- ½ teaspoon red curry paste

FOR THE THAI CURRY SAUCE

- 1 13.5-ounce (398 mL) can unsweetened coconut cream
- 1 tablespoon red curry paste
- Juice of 1 lime
- 2 garlic cloves, minced
- ¼ teaspoon sea salt

1. Preheat the oven to 350°F (180°C). Line 2 baking sheets with parchment paper.

2. In a large bowl, combine the chicken, cauliflower rice, onion, almond flour, cilantro, sesame oil, ginger, garlic, eggs, soy sauce, and curry paste. Use a spatula to fold everything together.

3. Using a small ice cream scoop or a tablespoon, form twenty-four 1- to 2-inch (3 to 5 cm) balls. Roll each ball between your hands to smooth out the edges and then place them on the prepared baking sheets, about 2 inches apart.

4. Bake one pan for 15 to 20 minutes, until the chicken is no longer pink and the meatballs have turned white with some areas of golden brown. Repeat with the second batch.

5. While the meatballs are baking, make the sauce: Pour the coconut cream into a large saucepan over medium heat. Whisk in the curry paste, lime juice, garlic, and salt. Bring to a boil, then reduce the heat and simmer for about 5 minutes. The sauce will thicken a bit. Transfer the baked meatballs to the saucepan and stir to coat with the sauce.

6. Serve with pasta, spaghetti squash, or spiralized veggies. Garnish with extra cilantro leaves, if using, and eat immediately.

7. To store leftover meatballs, place them in an airtight container along with the curry sauce and refrigerate for up to 1 week.

Note: In this recipe, you can use almond meal instead of the blanched almond flour if that's all you have on hand. Almond meal will give the meatballs a heartier, more granular, and nutty texture, but they will still taste delicious.

SWEET-AND-SOUR CAULIFLOWER

THIS DISH IS a lightened-up spin on a favorite Chinese takeout item. The sauce is a healthier version of sweet-and-sour sauce. You can coat the cauliflower pieces with tapioca flour, which adds a nice breading. Serve sweet-and-sour cauliflower with some sticky rice or roasted spaghetti squash to soak up all the extra sauce.

SERVES 2 TO 4

- 4 cups (540 g) medium cauliflower florets (see page 16)
- 2 tablespoons refined coconut oil, melted
- ¼ cup (34 g) tapioca flour

FOR THE SWEET-AND-SOUR SAUCE

- ⅓ cup (80 mL) cider vinegar
- ¼ cup (83 g) agave nectar, honey, or maple syrup (see Note, page 25)
- ¼ cup (59 g) ketchup
- 2 tablespoons tamari or soy sauce
- 1 garlic clove, minced
- 1 teaspoon grated fresh ginger
- ½ teaspoon onion powder

- 1 scallion, light green part only, chopped for garnish
- 1 teaspoon sesame seeds, for garnish

1. Preheat the oven to 425°F (220°C). Line a baking sheet with parchment paper.

2. Place the cauliflower florets and the coconut oil in a large plastic bag and shake until the florets are evenly coated with the oil. Add the tapioca flour to the bag. Shake again until the florets are coated with the flour.

3. Transfer the florets to the prepared baking sheet. Bake for about 30 minutes, until the florets begin to brown.

4. While the cauliflower is cooking, make the sauce: Place the vinegar, agave nectar, ketchup, tamari, garlic, ginger, and onion powder in a small pot over medium-high heat. Whisk for 3 minutes, until the mixture is smooth. Bring the sauce to a simmer and continue to cook for about 10 minutes, stirring frequently, until the sauce thickens.

5. Place the baked cauliflower in a bowl and toss with the sweet-and-sour sauce. Top with chopped scallions and sesame seeds and serve.

VEGETARIAN TACOS

....

SEASONED CAULIFLOWER AND walnuts make a tasty filling for vegetarian tacos (it can also fill lettuce wraps; see page 140). The nutty veggie combination is hearty, so you won't miss meat. Plus you can load the tacos with all the traditional toppings: salsa, corn, cheese—you name it! Use the taco filling for quesadillas, seven-layer dip, and even loaded nachos.

MAKES 6 TO 8 TACOS

FOR THE CAULIFLOWER FILLING

- 4 cups (420 g) cauliflower rice (see page 18)
- 2 cups (230 g) chopped walnuts
- 2 tablespoons refined coconut oil
- 2½ tablespoons homemade Taco Seasoning (page 115) or store-bought
- 6 to 8 tortillas

OPTIONAL TOPPINGS

- 2 ears of corn, shucked and silk removed
- 1 15-ounce (425 g) can black beans, drained and rinsed
- 1 cup (120 g) shredded Mexican cheese blend
- 1 avocado, sliced
- Salsa
- Cilantro leaves
- Lime, for serving

1. Combine the cauliflower rice, walnuts, and coconut oil in a large skillet over medium-high heat. Cook for 5 minutes, stirring frequently, until the cauliflower rice softens and appears translucent.

2. Add the Taco Seasoning to the pan and continue to cook, stirring constantly, for about 3 minutes, until the seasoning is well incorporated. Reduce the heat to low to keep the filling warm, stirring occasionally.

3. Heat a gas grill on high for 5 minutes, then reduce the heat to medium-low. Alternatively, prepare a charcoal grill with hot coals or place a grill pan over medium-high heat. Place the tortillas on top of a piece of aluminum foil or a grill mat (if using a grill) and cook until the edges of the tortillas are browned, about 3 minutes per side.

4. Place the shucked corn directly on the grill and cook for about 5 minutes, turning it occasionally, until it browns and has char marks. Remove the corn from the grill. When it is cool enough to handle, stand each ear up vertically on a cutting board and use a sharp knife to cut the kernels away from the cob.

5. To assemble the tacos, place some of the cauliflower filling inside each tortilla. Top with the corn, black beans, shredded cheese, avocado slices, salsa, cilantro, and lime, or the toppings of your choice.

6. Leftover taco filling can be stored in an airtight container in the fridge for up to 1 week.

CAULIFLOWER-WALNUT LETTUCE WRAPS

....

THESE ASIAN-INSPIRED LETTUCE wraps make an easy weeknight meal; they come together quickly and any leftovers make a convenient lunch the next day. Use green leaf lettuce for these wraps because not only does it have a great crunch, it also rolls and wraps without breaking. Can't find green leaf lettuce? Butter lettuce or romaine can serve as a substitute.

MAKES 6 TO 8 WRAPS

FOR THE FILLING

- 2 tablespoons avocado oil
- ½ sweet onion, chopped
- 1 red bell pepper, chopped
- 3 garlic cloves, minced
- 1 cup (100 g) walnuts
- 1⅔ cups (170 g) cauliflower rice (see page 18)
- ½ cup (114 g) water chestnuts, rinsed and coarsely chopped

FOR THE SAUCE

- 3 tablespoons tamari or soy sauce
- 1 tablespoon toasted sesame oil
- 1 tablespoon seasoned rice vinegar
- 1 tablespoon almond butter
- 1 tablespoon agave nectar (see Note, page 25)
- ½ teaspoon garlic powder
- ¼ teaspoon fish sauce
- ¼ teaspoon grated fresh ginger

1. Heat the avocado oil in a large skillet over medium-high heat. Add the onion and cook for 3 minutes. Add the bell pepper and garlic and continue to cook for about 7 minutes, until the onion is softened and starts to caramelize.

2. Pulse the walnuts in a food processor a couple of times until chopped to a granular consistency. Transfer the walnuts to the pan with the onion and bell pepper. Add the cauliflower rice and water chestnuts and cook for another 5 minutes, until the cauliflower begins to soften.

3. While the cauliflower mixture is cooking, make the sauce: Combine the tamari, sesame oil, vinegar, almond butter, agave nectar, garlic powder, fish sauce, and ginger in a jar. Secure the lid and shake the jar until the sauce is combined.

4. Stir about 3 tablespoons of the sauce into the cauliflower mixture and set the rest aside. Cook for another 2 to 3 minutes, until the sauce is well incorporated.

5. To assemble the lettuce wraps, scoop about ¼ cup of the cauliflower mixture onto each lettuce leaf. You might need more or less, depending on the size of the leaf. Make sure not to overfill the leaf. Roll the lettuce, tucking in the edges to fully enclose the filling.

- 6 to 8 leaves of green leaf lettuce

- 2 scallions, light green part only, chopped, for garnish

- 1 teaspoon sesame seeds, for garnish

- ⅓ cup (50 g) roasted cashews, coarsely chopped, for garnish

Top the wraps with chopped scallions, sesame seeds, and roasted cashews. Drizzle with the extra sauce or serve it on the side for dipping.

6. Store any leftover filling, lettuce, and sauce in separate airtight containers in the refrigerator so they can be assembled fresh another day.

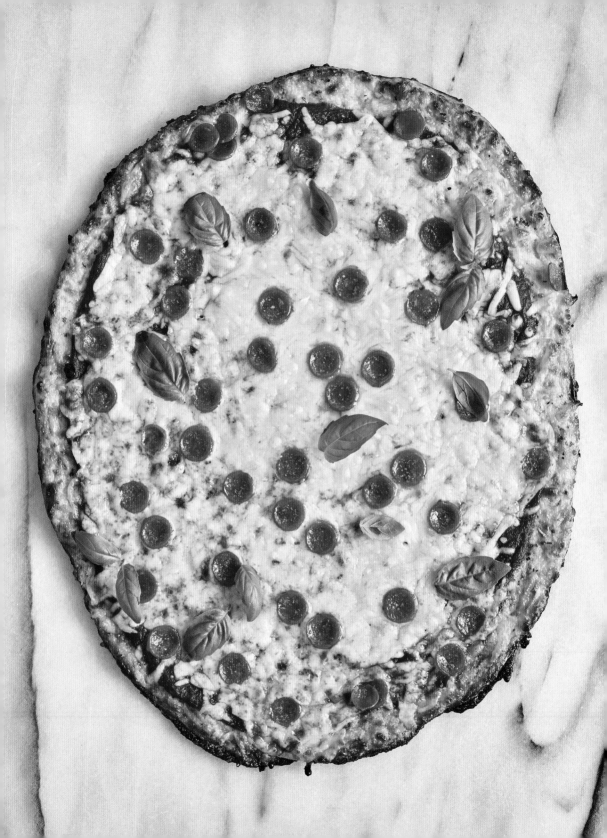

PIZZA

WITH A CAULIFLOWER CRUST

....

CAULIFLOWER PIZZA CRUST will make you realize that maybe cauliflower can do everything. I developed this low-glycemic pizza recipe for my husband, who has type 1 diabetes. But it's also a delicious alternative for those who are sensitive to gluten or have other dietary restrictions. When it comes to toppings, treat this crust as you would any pizza, which means the possibilities are endless. Try traditional cheese and pepperoni, but barbecued chicken and pepper Jack is one of my other favorite combinations (see the Variation).

SERVES 2 TO 4

FOR THE CRUST

- 3 cups (405 g) cauliflower florets (see page 16)
- 3 large eggs
- ½ cup (60 g) shredded Parmesan
- ½ cup (60 g) shredded mozzarella
- ½ teaspoon garlic powder
- ¼ teaspoon onion powder
- ¼ teaspoon dried basil
- ¼ teaspoon dried oregano
- ¼ teaspoon sea salt
- 1 tablespoon extra-virgin olive oil

FOR THE TOPPINGS

- 1 cup (120 mL) Pizza Sauce (recipe follows)
- 1 cup (120 g) shredded mozzarella
- ¼ cup (35 g) pepperoni
- ½ cup (20 g) fresh basil leaves

1. Preheat the oven to 450°F (230°C). Line a baking sheet with parchment paper.

2. Process the florets in a food processor until completely chopped into a fine meal (see page 19). You may need to do this in a couple of batches. After each batch is chopped, transfer it to a microwave-safe bowl.

3. Microwave the meal on high for 4 minutes. Alternatively, to prepare the cauliflower without a microwave, bring an inch of water to a boil in a medium saucepan. Place the florets in a steamer basket set over the boiling water. Cover and steam for about 5 minutes, until the florets are easily pierced with a fork. Remove the florets and let cool for 5 minutes. Place the steamed florets in a food processor and pulse until extra fine, resembling a meal.

4. Transfer the cauliflower meal to a clean, thin dish towel or piece of cheesecloth. Gather the ends and, working over the sink, squeeze out the excess liquid.

5. Place the squeezed cauliflower, eggs, Parmesan, mozzarella, garlic powder, onion powder, basil, oregano, and salt in a bowl and use a spatula to mix everything thoroughly. The mixture will appear mealy, but will hold together once cooked.

CONTINUED ....

6. Transfer the mixture to the baking sheet and use your hands to form it into a circle. You want the crust to be about ½ inch (1 cm) thick and 12 inches (30 cm) in diameter.

7. Drizzle or spray the crust with olive oil and bake for 15 minutes. After 15 minutes, if the center isn't golden brown, broil the crust on high for a couple of minutes to cook the center.

8. Remove the crust from the oven and spread the sauce over the top. Sprinkle with the shredded mozzarella and top with the pepperoni. Bake for another 10 minutes. Allow the pizza to stand for 4 minutes before garnishing with fresh basil and cutting it into slices.

9. Leftovers will keep in the refrigerator for about a week. Wrap them up or place them in an airtight container with layers of parchment paper between each slice to prevent them from sticking together.

VARIATION

BARBECUED CHICKEN PIZZA

Cook the crust as directed in the main recipe. Place 2 cups (250 g) cubed cooked chicken in a medium bowl and toss with ½ cup (120 mL) barbecue sauce. Spread another ½ cup (120 mL) of barbecue sauce across the cooked crust. Scatter 2 cups (240 g) shredded pepper Jack cheese on top, along with the barbecued chicken. Bake for an additional 10 minutes. Allow the pizza to stand for 4 minutes before garnishing with chopped fresh cilantro and cutting it into slices.

PIZZA SAUCE

MAKES 2 CUPS (240 ML)

- 1 15-ounce (425 g) can fire-roasted crushed tomatoes
- 3 tablespoons tomato paste
- 3 garlic cloves, minced
- 1 tablespoon agave nectar, honey, or maple syrup (see Note, page 25)
- 1 tablespoon dried oregano
- 1 tablespoon dried Italian seasoning

In a small bowl, whisk together the crushed tomatoes, tomato paste, garlic, agave nectar, oregano, and Italian seasoning. Use immediately or store in an airtight container in the refrigerator for up to 1 week.

GARLIC-HERB BUTTER GNOCCHI

GARLIC-HERB BUTTER GNOCCHI are a lightened-up version of the pasta traditionally made with potato. Using cauliflower in place of the potato makes for a lower-carb and lower-calorie gnocchi that can be a blank slate for your favorite sauce. Because cauliflower is not as starchy as potatoes, the batter is less doughy and not as malleable. The best way to achieve the iconic gnocchi shape is with a piping bag. This butter, garlic, and herb pasta sauce is classic, but you could also top the gnocchi with Kale Pesto (page 79), Sweet Basil Marinara Sauce (page 113), or Avocado-Cilantro Sauce (page 194) to switch it up.

MAKES 40 TO 50 GNOCCHI; SERVES 2

FOR THE GNOCCHI

- 2 cups (270 g) cauliflower florets (see page 16)
- ½ cup (60 g) grated Parmesan
- 2 tablespoons tapioca flour
- 1 large egg
- 1 large egg yolk

FOR THE GARLIC-HERB BUTTER SAUCE

- 4 tablespoons (½ stick/57 g) unsalted butter
- 2 garlic cloves, minced
- 1 tablespoon chopped fresh sage leaves
- 1 tablespoon chopped fresh chives
- ¼ cup (30 g) shredded Parmesan, plus more for garnish

1. Preheat the oven to 300°F (150°C). Line a baking sheet with parchment paper.

2. Process the florets in a food processor until completely chopped into meal (see page 19). Transfer the meal to a clean, thin dish towel or piece of cheesecloth and, working over the sink, squeeze out all the excess liquid.

3. Place the squeezed meal back in the food processor along with the Parmesan, tapioca flour, egg, and egg yolk. Process until the mixture is well combined and looks like a mash.

4. Transfer the mixture to a plastic baggie and cut off a corner to create a ½-inch (1 cm) opening. On the prepared baking sheet, pipe the gnocchi into pieces about 1 inch (3 cm) long and ½ inch (1 cm) to ¾ inch (2 cm) wide. The gnocchi won't spread too much while they cook, so you can line them up closely, about an inch (3 cm) apart.

5. Once all the gnocchi are piped, use your fingers to shape them gently into ovals. Then gently press the tops with a fork to get that traditional "lined" look. Bake for 30 minutes.

6. When the gnocchi are done, make the sauce: Heat the butter over medium-high heat in a pan large enough to hold the gnocchi. Add the garlic, sage, and chives. Cook for 2 minutes, until fragrant.

7. Add the baked gnocchi to the pan and toss a couple times until they are coated with the butter sauce. Add the ¼ cup Parmesan and cook for 1 minute more, allowing the cheese to melt and become integrated into the gnocchi. Sprinkle with additional Parmesan and serve immediately.

8. Leftovers can be kept in an airtight container in the fridge for about a week.

MOZZARELLA CHICKEN

THIS ONE-SKILLET DISH might remind you of chicken Parmesan. A cauliflower breading gives the chicken a crispy, crunchy outer layer that tastes like the real deal. Top the chicken with sun-dried tomato pesto and some mozzarella that gets browned until bubbly. It makes for a hearty, comforting dish that is family friendly and perfect for an easy weeknight meal.

SERVES 4

FOR THE CHICKEN

- 1 pound (454 g) skinless chicken breasts (3 or 4 pieces)
- 1 large egg
- ⅓ cup (42 g) Cauliflower Breading (recipe follows)
- 3 tablespoons salted butter
- 1 onion, chopped
- 6 garlic cloves, minced
- 1 15-ounce (425 g) can fire-roasted diced tomatoes
- ½ teaspoon sea salt
- ¼ teaspoon chipotle chile powder
- 8 ounces (227 g) mozzarella, sliced ½ inch thick

FOR THE SUN-DRIED TOMATO PESTO

- ⅓ cup (85 g) oil-packed sun-dried tomatoes, drained
- 1 tablespoon oil from the sun-dried tomato jar
- ¼ cup (31 g) pine nuts, toasted
- ½ cup (20 g) fresh basil leaves
- 1 garlic clove
- ½ teaspoon sea salt
- Fresh thyme leaves, for garnish

1. Preheat the oven to 350°F (180°C). Position one oven rack in the middle and another below the broiler.

2. Place the chicken breasts between 2 sheets of wax paper and pound with a meat tenderizer to an even thickness, about 1 inch (3 cm).

3. Whisk the egg in a shallow bowl. Place the Cauliflower Breading in a second shallow bowl. Dip each chicken breast in the egg to coat and then in the breading, making sure it's fully covered on both sides. Place the chicken on a plate and set aside. Repeat with the remaining pieces.

4. Melt 2 tablespoons of the butter in a large ovenproof skillet over medium-high heat. Place all the coated chicken in the pan and cook for 1 to 2 minutes, until golden brown and crispy on the bottom. Flip and cook the second side for another minute or two. You want the chicken to develop a nice crust. Transfer to a clean plate and set aside.

5. Melt the remaining tablespoon of butter in the same pan. Add the onion and garlic and cook for 7 minutes, stirring occasionally, until the onion is translucent and caramelized. Add the tomatoes, salt, and chipotle chile powder and whisk until well combined. Cook for another 3 minutes, return the chicken breasts to the pan, and remove from the heat.

CONTINUED

6. Make the pesto: Place the sun-dried tomatoes, oil, pine nuts, basil, garlic, and salt in a food processor. Process for 20 seconds, stopping halfway through to scrape down the sides with a rubber spatula.

7. Put a dollop of the sun-dried tomato pesto and slices of mozzarella on top of each chicken breast. Bake for 15 minutes, then broil for about 2 minutes or until the mozzarella gets bubbly and golden brown. Sprinkle with thyme leaves.

8. Serve with your favorite pasta or Garlic-Parmesan Cauliflower Rice (page 173). Leftovers can be kept in an airtight container in the fridge for up to 1 week. To reheat, cover loosely with foil and warm in a 300°F (150°C) oven for about 5 minutes or until just heated through.

CAULIFLOWER BREADING

CAULIFLOWER BREADING IS a great substitute for traditional breading. Whether you're making crispy chicken or sprinkling it on top of homestyle mac and cheese, there are endless ways to use it. Switch up the spices to make a barbecue-flavored or jerk-flavored seasoning.

MAKES ABOUT ½ CUP

- 5 cups (525 g) cauliflower rice (see page 18)
- ½ teaspoon dried basil
- ¼ teaspoon garlic powder
- ¼ teaspoon onion powder
- ¼ teaspoon dried oregano
- ¼ teaspoon dried thyme
- ¼ teaspoon sea salt
- ⅛ teaspoon freshly ground black pepper

1. Preheat the oven to 275°F (135°C). Line a baking sheet with parchment paper.

2. Spread the cauliflower rice evenly across the prepared baking sheet and bake for about 2 hours, until the rice is golden brown and toasted. Use a spatula or wooden spoon to stir every 30 minutes so it toasts evenly and doesn't burn.

3. Once the rice is dehydrated and lightly toasted, remove it from the oven and set aside to cool to room temperature.

4. Sprinkle the cooled rice with the basil, garlic powder, onion powder, oregano, thyme, salt, and pepper. Pour all the ingredients into a food processor with a blade attachment and process until combined and chopped into smaller pieces, about 1 minute. The breading consistency won't change drastically. The food processor will break down the rice so that the breading is more uniform, but it will generally stay about the same size. Use immediately, or store in an airtight container in the refrigerator for up to 3 weeks.

VARIATIONS

To make barbecue-flavored breading, swap out the herbs for these seasonings:

- 2 tablespoons coconut sugar
- 1 teaspoon garlic powder
- 1 teaspoon onion powder
- 1 teaspoon chili powder
- ½ teaspoon cayenne pepper
- ½ teaspoon smoked paprika
- ½ teaspoon ground cumin
- ½ teaspoon sea salt
- ¼ teaspoon freshly ground black pepper

To make jerk-flavored breading, replace the herbs with these seasonings:

- 1 teaspoon onion powder
- 1 teaspoon cayenne pepper
- 1 teaspoon dried thyme
- 1 teaspoon coconut sugar
- ½ teaspoon garlic powder
- ½ teaspoon smoked paprika
- ½ teaspoon ground allspice
- ¼ teaspoon red pepper flakes
- ¼ teaspoon ground cinnamon
- ¼ teaspoon grated nutmeg

CAULIFLOWER CHILI

WHEN THE AIR turns a little crisp come September and October, there's nothing more satisfying and comforting than a pot of chili. It's a hearty meal that becomes more flavorful after a day or two, which means it's even better when eaten as leftovers. Here cauliflower florets stand in for meat, maintaining the hearty and flavorful quality that everyone loves in a chili.

SERVES 6

- 2 tablespoons avocado oil
- 2 cups (270 g) small to medium cauliflower florets (see page 16)
- 1 large sweet potato, cut into ½- to 1-inch (1 to 3 cm) pieces
- 1 yellow onion, coarsely chopped
- 3 garlic cloves, minced
- 1 28-ounce (794 g) can fire-roasted diced tomatoes
- 1 15-ounce (425 g) can black beans, drained and rinsed
- 2 tablespoons chili powder
- 4 teaspoons ground cumin
- ½ teaspoon chipotle chile powder
- ¼ teaspoon sea salt

OPTIONAL TOPPINGS

- Sour cream
- ½ cup fresh or frozen and thawed corn kernels
- Chopped fresh cilantro
- Avocado slices
- Shredded Cheddar

1. Heat the avocado oil in a large pot over medium-high heat. Add the cauliflower, sweet potato, and onion and cook for about 10 minutes, stirring occasionally, until the veggies begin to soften and the onion starts to brown.

2. Add the garlic and cook for another 3 minutes.

3. Add 2½ cups (600 mL) water, the diced tomatoes, black beans, chili powder, cumin, chipotle chile powder, and salt. Bring to a boil, then reduce the heat to maintain a gentle simmer. Cook for another 5 to 10 minutes, until the chili thickens a bit and is less watery.

4. Transfer to individual bowls and serve with the desired toppings: sour cream, corn, cilantro, avocado slices, and Cheddar. The chili will keep stored in an airtight container in the fridge for about a week.

SWEET POTATO CAULIFLOWER CURRY BOATS

CAULIFLOWER AND CURRY are a magical pairing where the curry brings all the flavor and heat. You can use red curry paste to add a nice level of spice to the cauliflower filling, but you can easily substitute yellow curry if you prefer something milder. Curry is a great meal for leftovers because the flavors intensify when stored overnight in the fridge. Make a big batch ahead of time, roast the sweet potatoes when you're ready to eat, and this meal will come together with hardly any effort. Look for wider, round sweet potatoes instead of long skinny ones. The wider ones make for better boats!

SERVES 6

- 3 large sweet potatoes
- 3 tablespoons avocado oil
- 2½ cups (338 g) small cauliflower florets (see page 16)
- ½ onion, diced
- 1 cup (165 g) canned chickpeas, drained and rinsed
- 1 13.5-ounce (398 mL) can unsweetened coconut cream
- 1 tablespoon red curry paste
- Juice of ½ lime
- 1 tablespoon coconut nectar, agave nectar, honey, or maple syrup (see Note, page 25)
- 1 tablespoon natural peanut butter
- 1 tablespoon soy sauce
- 2 garlic cloves, minced
- Fresh cilantro leaves, for garnish

1. Preheat the oven to 400°F (200°C). Line a baking sheet with parchment paper.

2. Cut the sweet potatoes in half lengthwise and rub them with 1 tablespoon of the avocado oil. Place them flat side down on the prepared baking sheet. Roast for 30 minutes or until the flesh is tender when pricked with a fork and the outer skin is wrinkly.

3. While the potatoes are roasting, make the curry: Heat the remaining 2 tablespoons avocado oil in a large skillet over medium-high heat. Add the cauliflower and onion and cook for 10 minutes, stirring frequently, until the onion becomes translucent and the veggies begin to caramelize.

4. Add the chickpeas to the pan and cook for 2 minutes. Add the coconut cream, curry paste, lime juice, coconut nectar, peanut butter, soy sauce, and garlic. Stir to completely combine. Reduce the heat to medium-low and continue to cook for 5 minutes, until the sauce thickens a bit.

5. When the sweet potatoes are roasted, cut down the center of each to expose more of the the flesh. Use a fork to mash up the flesh. Add a scoop of the cauliflower curry on top, and garnish with cilantro leaves.

FETTUCCINE ALFREDO

WHENEVER I WANT an easy meal that can please the whole family, I make an Alfredo. The kids love the cheesy sauce, and when I make it with sweet potato noodles, I know it's good for them too—a win-win. The steamed cauliflower makes this sauce extra creamy and pairs beautifully with any noodle, from spiralized sweet potato to a traditional fettuccine, or even a chickpea noodle.

SERVES 4 TO 6

- 3 cups (405 g) cauliflower florets (see page 16)
- 1 cup (120 g) shredded Parmesan
- ¾ cup (180 mL) heavy cream
- 2 ounces (57 g) cream cheese
- 2 tablespoons salted butter
- 2 garlic cloves
- ¼ teaspoon sea salt
- ¼ teaspoon freshly ground black pepper, plus more for serving
- 1 pound (454 g) dried fettuccine, Sweet Potato Noodles (recipe follows), or other pasta of your choice

1. Bring an inch of water to a boil in a medium saucepan. Place the cauliflower florets in a steamer basket set over the boiling water. Cover and steam for about 5 minutes, until the florets are tender.

2. Transfer the steamed florets to a high-powered blender along with the Parmesan, heavy cream, cream cheese, butter, garlic, salt, and pepper. Blend on high until smooth and creamy, about 1 minute.

3. If using pasta, bring a large pot of salted water to a boil. Cook the fettuccine according to the package directions, then drain.

4. In a large saucepan over medium-high heat, heat the sauce from the blender until it begins to bubble, about 5 minutes. Add the fettuccine to the pan and toss with tongs to coat. (Alternatively, you could plate the noodles and pour the hot Alfredo sauce over them.)

5. Serve hot with a sprinkle of additional ground pepper, if desired. Leftovers will keep for about a week in an airtight container in the fridge.

SWEET POTATO NOODLES

MAKES 4 CUPS

- 2 large sweet potatoes, washed and peeled
- 1 tablespoon refined coconut oil

1. Turn the sweet potatoes into noodles using the fettuccine blade on a spiralizer.

2. Melt the coconut oil over medium-high heat in a large skillet and add the sweet potato noodles. Use tongs to toss the noodles for 3 minutes. Add 1 tablespoon water and continue to toss for another 2 minutes, until the noodles are tender but not falling apart—they should still be al dente.

3. Serve with Alfredo sauce, Avocado-Cilantro Sauce (page 194), Sun-Dried Tomato Pesto (page 148), or Kale Pesto (page 79). Leftovers can be kept in an airtight container in the fridge for up to 1 week.

ONE-PAN LEMON SAGE CHICKEN AND CAULIFLOWER

ONE-PAN DINNERS MEAN an even faster cleanup on a busy weeknight. Here the chicken is cooked with a creamy, lemony sauce that is so good you'll want to spoon it over the cauliflower, too.

SERVES 2 TO 4

- 1 pound (454 g) boneless, skinless chicken thighs
- 1 tablespoon smoked paprika
- 1 teaspoon sea salt
- 1 teaspoon freshly ground black pepper
- 3 tablespoons salted butter
- 3 cups (405 g) cauliflower florets (see page 16)
- 3 garlic cloves, minced
- ½ cup (120 mL) chicken broth
- ½ cup (120 mL) heavy cream
- ⅓ cup (40 g) shredded Parmesan
- Juice of 1 lemon, plus slices, for garnish (optional)
- 1 tablespoon chopped fresh sage leaves

1. Preheat the oven to 350°F (180°C).

2. Season the chicken on both sides with the paprika, salt, and pepper.

3. In a large ovenproof skillet, melt 2 tablespoons of the butter over medium-high heat. Add the chicken and sear on both sides until golden brown, 2 to 3 minutes per side. Remove the chicken and set aside on a clean plate.

4. Add the remaining tablespoon of butter to the pan and cook the cauliflower and garlic for about 3 minutes, stirring occasionally, until browned.

5. Stir in the chicken broth, heavy cream, Parmesan, lemon juice, and sage. Cook until the sauce begins to bubble, about 5 minutes. Nestle the chicken back in the pan, transfer to the oven, and roast for 15 minutes, or until the chicken is cooked through and no longer pink in the center.

6. To serve, place one chicken thigh and some cauliflower in a shallow bowl and spoon the sauce from the pan over the top with more lemon, if desired. Leftovers can be kept in an airtight container in the fridge for up to 1 week.

GRILLED CAULIFLOWER STEAKS

WITH PARSNIP MASH AND GRAVY

THIS VEGETARIAN TWIST on steak and mashed potatoes will leave even an ardent meat eater satisfied. Grilling the cauliflower steaks adds great flavor to this dish and makes cauliflower all the more convincing as a meat alternative. If you don't have a grill, you can use a grill pan and cook the steaks on your stovetop, or roast them in the oven (see page 15). The recipe uses beef broth in the gravy, but to keep it completely vegetarian, you can substitute vegetable broth.

SERVES 4

FOR THE GRAVY

- 4 cups (1 L) beef broth
- 2 teaspoons cream of tartar
- 2 tablespoons arrowroot flour (see Note, page 93)
- 1 tablespoon Worcestershire sauce
- 1 teaspoon garlic powder
- 1 teaspoon onion powder

FOR THE PARSNIP MASH

- 4 large parsnips
- 8 garlic cloves
- ½ cup (120 mL) extra-virgin olive oil
- Sea salt and freshly ground black pepper

(continued)

1. Prepare a charcoal grill with hot coals or heat a gas grill on the high setting for 10 minutes. Alternatively, heat a grill pan on the stovetop over high heat.

2. Meanwhile, make the gravy: Pour the broth into a medium saucepan over medium-low heat. Add the cream of tartar and arrowroot flour to the broth, whisking continuously until they dissolve. Add the Worcestershire sauce, garlic powder, and onion powder. Turn the heat to high and bring to a boil, then reduce the heat to low. Simmer the gravy for about 30 minutes, whisking frequently, until it thickens.

3. Make the mash: Peel the parsnips and cut off the rough ends. Cut the parsnips into ½-inch (1 cm) rounds and then cut each round in half to make half-moons.

4. Bring an inch of water to a boil in a medium saucepan. Place the parsnips and garlic in a steamer basket set over the boiling water. Cover and steam for about 10 minutes, until the parsnips are tender.

5. Transfer the steamed parsnips and garlic to a high-powered blender along with the olive oil and salt and pepper to taste. Blend on high for about 1 minute,

FOR THE CAULIFLOWER STEAKS

- 4 cauliflower steaks (12 to 16 ounces/340 to 454 g each), cut from 1 to 2 heads of cauliflower (see page 15)
- 2 tablespoons avocado oil
- 1 teaspoon garlic powder
- 1 teaspoon coconut sugar
- ½ teaspoon dry mustard
- ¼ teaspoon chili powder
- ¼ teaspoon smoked paprika
- ¼ teaspoon ground cumin
- ¼ teaspoon sea salt
- ¼ teaspoon freshly ground black pepper
- 1 tablespoon chopped fresh chives, for garnish

until creamy and smooth. Set aside. The mash will already be warm from steaming, but you could keep it warm, covered, in a pot set over low heat while you grill the cauliflower.

6. Make the steaks: Drizzle the cauliflower steaks with the avocado oil. In a small bowl, mix the garlic powder, coconut sugar, mustard, chili powder, paprika, cumin, salt, and pepper. Sprinkle the seasoning over the cauliflower steaks, making sure they're evenly coated. Flip the steaks and season the other side.

7. Lower the grill heat to medium or spread out the coals to create a medium heat zone. Set a grill mat or a piece of aluminum foil on the grill and lay the cauliflower steaks on top. Grill each steak for 8 minutes per side, until tender and charred.

8. Place a dollop of parsnip mash on each plate. Top with a cauliflower steak and drizzle with gravy. Sprinkle with chopped chives for garnish. The mash and steaks can be stored separately in airtight containers in the fridge for about 1 week.

VEGGIE BURGERS

WITH PEANUT SAUCE AND SLAW

THESE VEGGIE BURGERS can be made totally vegan if you prefer. Soaked flax meal can act as the binding agent for the cauliflower, chickpeas, and other burger ingredients. If you want to make vegetarian veggie burgers, skip the flax and add an egg to the burger mixture instead. Dress up the burgers with a crunchy slaw and peanut sauce or keep them simple and serve with some ketchup or avocado.

MAKES 6 BURGERS

FOR THE BURGERS

- 2½ tablespoons ground flax meal, or 2 large eggs
- 1 cup (105 g) cauliflower rice (see page 18)
- 1 cup (115 g) blanched almond flour (see Note, page 31)
- ½ cup (70 g) raw almonds, chopped
- ½ cup (75 g) chopped onion
- ½ cup (80 g) sunflower seeds
- ½ cup (83 g) canned chickpeas, drained and rinsed
- ¼ cup (10 g) fresh cilantro leaves
- 2 tablespoons avocado oil, plus more for the pan
- 1 tablespoon soy sauce
- 1½ teaspoons chipotle chile powder
- 1 teaspoon ground cumin
- ½ teaspoon sea salt

(continued)

1. Place the flax meal in ½ cup (120 mL) water, stir, and set aside for 5 minutes. The flax meal will expand and take on a jelly-like texture resembling that of an egg. If you are using eggs instead of the flax, beat the eggs in a small bowl and set aside.

2. In a large bowl, combine the cauliflower rice, almond flour, almonds, onion, sunflower seeds, chickpeas, cilantro, avocado oil, soy sauce, chipotle chile powder, cumin, and salt and mix well with a spatula.

3. Pour the soaked flax or beaten egg into the bowl and mix everything together until thoroughly combined. The flax meal will have absorbed most of the soaking water and become a thick mixture so you can pour the entire contents into the bowl. Allow to rest for 5 minutes.

4. Meanwhile, make the sauce: In a small bowl, whisk together the peanut butter, tamari, agave nectar, sesame oil, and hot sauce. Set aside.

5. Make the slaw: In a medium bowl, mix the green cabbage, red cabbage, carrot, mayonnaise, cilantro, garlic, hot sauce, and salt and pepper to taste. Set aside.

CONTINUED

FOR THE PEANUT SAUCE

- 1 tablespoon peanut butter
- 1 tablespoon tamari
- 1 tablespoon agave nectar (see Note, page 25)
- 1 teaspoon toasted sesame oil
- ½ teaspoon hot sauce

FOR THE SLAW

- ½ cup (75 g) finely shredded green cabbage
- ½ cup (75 g) finely shredded red cabbage
- 1 carrot, shredded
- ½ cup (108 g) mayonnaise, avocado oil mayonnaise, or vegan mayonnaise
- ¼ cup (10 g) chopped fresh cilantro leaves
- 2 garlic cloves, minced
- 1 teaspoon hot sauce
- Sea salt and freshly ground black pepper

- 6 burger buns, optional

6. Preheat the oven to 250°F (120°C). Line a baking sheet with parchment paper.

7. Use your hands to form 6 burger patties 3 to 4 inches (8 to 10 cm) in diameter and about ½ inch (1 cm) thick. Set aside on a clean plate.

8. Heat 2 tablespoons avocado oil in a large skillet over medium-high heat. Cook the burgers for about 3 minutes per side, until each side is golden brown. You should be able to fit 3 burgers in the pan at once.

9. To keep the cooked burgers warm while you cook the second batch, set them on the lined baking sheet and place in the low oven.

10. Serve the veggie burgers on buns loaded with slaw and a dollop of peanut sauce. Or go bunless and serve on a plate with the slaw and peanut sauce overtop.

SHEPHERD'S PIE

A HEARTY SHEPHERD'S pie loaded with meat and vegetables is the perfect cozy winter dish. Shepherd's pie also makes an awesome end-of-the-week meal because you can use whatever veggies you might have left in your fridge from the week. Add in some corn kernels, chopped celery, sweet potato cubes, peas—you name it! Here the lightened-up mash on top is made with cauliflower. It creates a creamy and fluffy layer that bakes up just like the traditional potatoes.

SERVES 4

FOR THE TOPPING

- 3 cups (405 g) cauliflower florets (see page 16)
- 3 tablespoons ghee, unsalted butter, or refined coconut oil
- 2 garlic cloves, minced
- ¼ teaspoon sea salt
- ⅛ teaspoon freshly ground black pepper

FOR THE FILLING

- 2 tablespoons ghee, butter, or coconut oil
- 1 sweet onion, coarsely chopped
- 2 garlic cloves, minced
- 2 large carrots, coarsely chopped
- 1 pound (454 g) grass-fed ground beef
- 1 tablespoon ketchup
- 1 tablespoon soy sauce (tamari for gluten-free)
- 1 tablespoon barbecue sauce
- ½ teaspoon sea salt
- 2 tablespoons chopped fresh chives

1. Preheat the oven to 350°F (180°C). Position one oven rack in the middle and another just below the broiler.

2. Fill a large pot with water and bring it to a boil over high heat. Add the florets and boil for 3 to 5 minutes, until they are easily pierced with a fork.

3. While the cauliflower is cooking, start the filling: Heat the 2 tablespoons ghee in a large skillet over medium heat. Add the onion and garlic. When the onion starts to soften, about 5 minutes, add the carrots. Continue to cook for about 10 minutes, stirring occasionally, until the onion is browned and translucent and the carrots are easily pierced with a fork.

4. Add the ground beef to the pan. Use a spatula to break it up into small pieces. Cook for about 5 minutes, until the meat is browned and no longer pink. Add the ketchup, soy sauce, barbecue sauce, and salt to the pan and stir.

5. Once the sauce incorporates into the dish and reduces, about 3 minutes, remove from the heat.

6. Make the topping: When the cauliflower is tender, drain it and place it in the food processor with the 3 tablespoons ghee, garlic, salt, and pepper. Process for 1 minute. Use a rubber spatula to scrape down the sides and process for another 30 seconds, until the cauliflower mash is completely smooth and creamy.

7. In an 8 by 8-inch (20 by 20 cm) square casserole dish, spread the cooked meat evenly over the bottom. Use a spatula to spread the cauliflower puree on top of the meat.

8. Bake for 20 minutes, until the edges are golden brown. Switch to the broiler setting and broil on high for 2 minutes to get the entire top of the pie golden brown. Sprinkle with fresh chopped chives and serve.

9. Scoop the shepherd's pie into bowls or plates and enjoy immediately. Leftovers can be kept in an airtight container in the fridge for about a week.

5

SIDES

CAULIFLOWER AS A dinner side dish is as traditional as you can get. But this chapter is all about transforming cauliflower into an exciting and innovative counterpart in its own right. In this chapter you'll find easy ways to substitute cauliflower rice for traditional rice to lighten up your meal. There's also a casserole that's easy enough for a weeknight but special enough for a holiday. Cauliflower is an unexpected ingredient in supporting players too—try the Garlic Naan, Cheddar-Jalapeño Cauliflower Biscuits, or Savory Churros with Garlic-Dijon Aïoli.

CAULIFLOWER RICE FIVE WAYS

ONCE YOU GET the hang of making cauliflower rice, you'll no doubt want to experiment with different flavor combinations. Here are my five go-to ways to season cauliflower rice. Coconut Cauliflower Rice is creamy and has a tropical taste. Serve it with some grilled fish and mango salsa. Cauliflower Fried Rice is great with Asian-inspired dishes, chicken kabobs, or even some simple sautéed shrimp. Turmeric Cauliflower Rice adds a punch of flavor and color to your meal. Serve it with some grilled chicken or tofu. The Garlic-Parmesan Cauliflower Rice is a straightforward rice to serve with a flavorsome main dish like a curry or even a traditional steak. Cilantro-Lime Cauliflower Rice is light and citrusy, which makes it a good balance for heavier dishes like grilled meat or a stew.

COCONUT CAULIFLOWER RICE

MAKES ABOUT 4 CUPS

- 2 tablespoons refined coconut oil
- 3 cups (315 g) cauliflower rice (see page 18)
- 1 13.5-ounce (398 mL) can full-fat unsweetened coconut milk, chilled
- 1 cup (85 g) unsweetened shredded coconut
- Sea salt

1. In a large skillet over medium-high heat, stir together the coconut oil and the cauliflower rice. After about 3 minutes, open the can of chilled coconut milk. The thick white cream will be at the top and the silky translucent milk will be on the bottom. Scoop out the layer of white cream and stir it into the cauliflower. Discard the remaining coconut milk, or refrigerate it for use in a different recipe.

2. Allow the cauliflower rice to simmer for about 3 minutes, or until all the coconut milk has been absorbed and the rice is soft and thickened.

3. Add the shredded coconut and continue to cook over low heat, stirring occasionally, for about 5 to 10 minutes, until you are ready to use the rice. Add sea salt to taste. Leftovers can be stored in an airtight container in the fridge for up to a week.

1. Turmeric / 2. Garlic-Parmesan / 3. Cilantro-Lime (also pictured on page 175) / 4. Coconut / 5. Fried (also pictured on page 172)

CONTINUED

CAULIFLOWER FRIED RICE

MAKES 4 CUPS

- 4 tablespoons (60 mL) toasted sesame oil
- ⅓ cup (41 g) shredded carrot
- ½ red bell pepper, chopped
- ⅓ cup (40 g) frozen peas
- 3 cups (315 g) cauliflower rice (see page 18)
- 1 garlic clove, minced
- ¾ cup (180 mL) soy sauce
- 2 large eggs, whisked
- 1 scallion, white and light green parts, chopped
- 1 teaspoon black sesame seeds

1. In a large skillet over medium-high heat, combine 2 tablespoons of the sesame oil, the carrot, bell pepper, and frozen peas. Cook for about 10 minutes, until the peppers are softened and slightly browned and the peas are bright green.

2. Add the cauliflower rice, garlic, and ½ cup (120 mL) of the soy sauce, stirring frequently until the rice is tender, 3 to 5 minutes.

3. Add the whisked eggs and stir constantly until the eggs are scrambled throughout the rice.

4. Add the remaining ¼ cup (60 mL) soy sauce and remaining 2 tablespoons sesame oil. Stir to combine and remove from the heat. Top with the chopped scallion and sesame seeds and serve. Leftovers can be stored in an airtight container in the fridge for up to a week.

GARLIC-PARMESAN CAULIFLOWER RICE

MAKES 3 CUPS

- 1 tablespoon salted butter
- 1 shallot, finely chopped
- 6 garlic cloves, minced
- 3 cups (315 g) cauliflower rice (see page 18)
- ½ cup (60 g) shredded Parmesan
- 1 tablespoon chopped fresh chives
- Sea salt and freshly ground black pepper

1. Melt the butter in a large skillet over medium-high heat and add the shallot and garlic. Cook for 2 minutes, then add the cauliflower rice. Cook for 10 minutes, stirring frequently, until specks of the rice are slightly browned.

2. Add the Parmesan, chives, and salt and pepper to taste. Stir for another couple of minutes, until the cheese melts. Serve immediately. Store leftovers in an airtight container in the fridge for up to a week.

CONTINUED

TURMERIC CAULIFLOWER RICE

MAKES ABOUT 3 CUPS

- 1 sweet onion, chopped
- 1 tablespoon avocado oil
- 2 garlic cloves, minced
- 3 cups (315 g) cauliflower rice (see page 18)
- 1 teaspoon turmeric
- ½ teaspoon sea salt
- ¼ teaspoon freshly ground black pepper
- ⅓ cup (54 g) dried cranberries
- ⅓ cup (28 g) sliced almonds, toasted
- ½ cup (20 g) chopped fresh herbs such as parsley or cilantro

1. In a large skillet over medium-high heat, combine the onion and avocado oil. Cook, stirring frequently, for about 5 minutes, until the onion is soft and translucent.

2. Add the garlic and continue to cook for another 3 to 5 minutes until the onions are golden brown. Add the cauliflower rice and cook until it has softened, about 3 minutes.

3. Add the turmeric, salt, and pepper and continue to cook for another 2 minutes.

4. Toss in the cranberries, almonds, and herbs. Stir to combine, then remove from heat and serve. Leftovers can be stored in an airtight container in the fridge for up to 1 week.

CILANTRO-LIME CAULIFLOWER RICE

MAKES 3 CUPS

- 1 tablespoon avocado oil
- ½ onion, finely chopped
- 2 garlic cloves, minced
- 3 cups (315 g) cauliflower rice (see page 18)
- ½ cup (20 g) fresh cilantro leaves, plus more for garnish (optional)
- 3 tablespoons lime juice (about 2 limes)
- 1 tablespoon seasoned rice vinegar
- 1 tablespoon coconut nectar, agave nectar, honey, or maple syrup (see Note, page 25)
- ½ teaspoon sea salt

1. Heat the avocado oil in a skillet over medium-high heat. Add the onion and garlic and cook, stirring frequently, for about 5 minutes, until the onion turns translucent.

2. Reduce the heat to medium, add the cauliflower rice, and continue to cook for another 5 minutes, until the rice softens.

3. Meanwhile, place the cilantro, lime juice, rice vinegar, coconut nectar, and salt in a food processor. Process for about 15 seconds, until combined.

4. Add the cilantro-lime sauce to the pan with the cauliflower rice and cook for another 5 minutes, until the excess liquid has evaporated. Garnish with more cilantro leaves, if using. Serve immediately. Store leftovers in an airtight container in the fridge for up to 1 week.

PICKLED CAULIFLOWER

YOU MAY FIND yourself from time to time with leftover cauliflower that you don't want to waste. One option is ricing and freezing it so you can make smoothies the next morning (see page 26). Another option is to quick pickle it. Eat pickled cauliflower on its own or use it as a topping for salads or toast. Any color of cauliflower will do!

MAKES 1 CUP

- 1 cup (135 g) cauliflower florets (see page 16)
- 1 cup (240 mL) cider vinegar
- 1 tablespoon agave nectar, honey, or maple syrup (see Note, page 25)
- 1 garlic clove, minced
- ½ teaspoon sea salt
- ½ teaspoon black peppercorns or mustard seeds (optional)

1. Place the florets in a lidded container. A 2-pint (1 L) Mason jar works well. Be sure to leave some space at the top for the pickling liquid.

2. In a small saucepan over medium-high heat, warm the vinegar, agave nectar, garlic, and salt. Whisking frequently, let simmer for 5 minutes.

3. Pour the cider mixture into the container, add the peppercorns or mustard seeds, if using, and allow the contents to come to room temperature.

4. Use a spoon to push the florets down; you want them to be submerged in the vinegar mixture.

5. Secure the lid and refrigerate for at least 24 hours. The pickled florets will keep for about 1 month.

SWEET POTATO– CAULIFLOWER SOUP

THE GORGEOUS ORANGE color of this soup is a showstopper. You get the rich hue by pairing orange cauliflower with sweet potato. Of course, you can make this soup with whatever color vegetables you have available. Aesthetically speaking, purple sweet potato would go great with white or purple cauliflower. Mixing the vegetable colors *might* result in a visually unappetizing soup, though it'll still taste good. For a tasty party appetizer, serve this soup in shot glasses to make soup shooters. Topping the soup with coconut cream, minced garlic, and thyme leaves adds an immediate fragrant flavor to the soup that you can customize to your tastebuds. Consider adding some texture to the soup by topping with chickpea croutons (page 84), crumbled cheese, chopped bacon, or sautéed mushrooms.

MAKES 6 CUPS

- 3 cups (405 g) orange cauliflower florets (see page 16)
- 1 small sweet potato, peeled and cut into 1-inch (3 cm) pieces
- 1 yellow onion, coarsely chopped
- 8 garlic cloves
- 2 tablespoons extra-virgin olive oil
- Sea salt and freshly ground black pepper
- 1 cup (142 g) raw cashews
- 2 cups (480 mL) vegetable stock
- ½ cup (120 mL) unsweetened coconut cream
- 1 tablespoon fresh thyme leaves, for garnish

1. Preheat the oven to 400°F (200°C). Line a baking sheet with parchment paper.

2. Place the florets, sweet potato, onion, and 4 of the garlic cloves on the baking sheet. Drizzle with olive oil and sprinkle with salt and pepper to taste. Use your hands to mix the vegetables with the oil until coated. Roast for 40 minutes, until tender and lightly browned.

3. While the vegetables are roasting, bring a small pot of water to a boil. Add the cashews and boil for about 10 minutes, until softened. (Alternatively, if you plan ahead, you can soak the cashews overnight in a jar of water in your fridge and skip the boiling step.) Drain the cashews, discarding the water, and place in a high-powered blender along with the vegetable stock and 1 cup fresh water.

4. Add the roasted vegetables to the blender and blend on high until smooth and combined, about 2 minutes. Depending on the size of your blender, you may need to do this in batches. Pour the soup into a large pot set

over high heat and bring to a boil to warm the soup through.

5. Place the coconut cream in a small bowl and microwave for 30 seconds until smooth and drizzly. You can also just warm the coconut cream on the stovetop.

6. Pour the soup into serving bowls. Mince the remaining 4 garlic cloves. Top each bowl with a drizzle of coconut cream, 1 teaspoon minced garlic, a sprinkle of salt and pepper, and fresh thyme leaves. Leftovers can be stored in an airtight container in the fridge for about 1 week. Reheat in the microwave or in a pan on the stove, stirring frequently.

WHOLE ROASTED CAULIFLOWER

WITH SUN-DRIED TOMATO AND SESAME

ALTHOUGH YOU CAN likely think of a million ways to use this sun-dried-tomato topping (like on some toast with slices of avocado, or tossed in a pasta salad, or mixed in your scrambled eggs), coating the whole cauliflower head and roasting it is one of the most satisfying. It smells amazing while it's in the oven, plus a whole roasted head of cauliflower is a total "wow" moment when you bring it to the table. Once the cauliflower has had its moment of presentation, use a knife to cut off wedges and serve.

SERVES 6

- 1 large head cauliflower (see page 14)
- ½ cup (51 g) white sesame seeds
- 1 cup (215 g) drained, oil-packed sun-dried tomatoes
- 3 tablespoons extra-virgin olive oil
- ½ cup (20 g) fresh flat-leaf parsley leaves
- 3 garlic cloves, minced
- ½ teaspoon smoked paprika
- ½ teaspoon sea salt
- ¼ teaspoon sumac (see Note)

1. Preheat the oven to 400°F (200°C).

2. Remove and discard the leaves from the head of the cauliflower, and cut away some of the stem so the cauliflower can sit flat on a cutting board. Handle the head carefully so that it stays fully intact.

3. Bring a large pot of water to a boil. Boil the whole head of cauliflower for 7 minutes, turning it after 4 minutes. Drain the cauliflower and pat dry.

4. Place the sesame seeds in a small skillet over medium-high heat. Toast the seeds, stirring frequently, for about 5 minutes, until they become fragrant and golden.

5. Combine the toasted sesame seeds, sun-dried tomatoes, 2 tablespoons of the olive oil, the parsley, garlic, paprika, salt, and sumac in a food processor. Process on high for 30 seconds. Use a rubber spatula to scrape down the sides and process again for another 30 seconds, until the topping is finely chopped and well combined.

CONTINUED

6. Drizzle the remaining tablespoon of olive oil in the bottom of a large ovenproof skillet. Working off the heat, place the cauliflower head in the skillet. Starting from the underside of the cauliflower, use your hands to spread and press the sun-dried tomato topping into all the cracks and crevices.

7. Once the bottom is coated, flip the cauliflower so it's sitting flat and upright in the skillet. Continue to spread and press the topping into the cauliflower head until it is coated and all the topping is used. If any topping falls into the skillet, pick it up and press it back onto the cauliflower head.

8. Place the skillet in the oven and roast for 40 minutes, until golden brown. After 40 minutes, raise the temperature to 500°F (260°C) and roast for another 10 minutes, until the outside is toasted and crisp.

Note: Sumac is a spice used often in Middle Eastern and South Asian cuisines. The sumac bush produces red berries that are dried and ground up into a coarse powder. Sumac has a tangy, lemony flavor but is less tart than straight lemon juice. Use it in rubs, marinades, and dressings, or sprinkle some on top of a finished dish for a pop of red color and a tart finish.

CREAMY CAULIFLOWER MAC AND CHEESE

I HAVE YET to meet a person who doesn't love macaroni and cheese. This homemade version is a great opportunity to sneak extra veggies into your meals. If you can't eat almonds, leave out the nutty topping. It adds a nice texture to the top, but the casserole is equally good without it.

SERVES 8

- 1 pound (454 g) elbow chickpea pasta
- 2 cups (210 g) cauliflower rice (see page 18)
- ½ cup (120 mL) whole milk
- 2 cups (240 g) shredded Cheddar
- 3 garlic cloves
- ½ teaspoon sea salt
- 1 cup (140 g) whole raw almonds
- 1 tablespoon refined coconut oil
- 1 tablespoon agave nectar, honey, or maple syrup (see Note, page 25)
- Fresh parsley leaves, for garnish

1. Cook the pasta according to the package directions.

2. Bring an inch of water to a boil in a medium saucepan. Place the cauliflower rice in a steamer basket set over the boiling water. Cover and steam for 5 minutes, until the cauliflower has softened and is translucent around the edges.

3. Place the steamed cauliflower rice, milk, Cheddar, garlic, and salt in a high-powdered blender and blend until completely smooth and creamy.

4. When the pasta is al dente, drain it and place the macaroni back in the pot. Pour the sauce into the pot and stir to combine.

5. You can serve the mac and cheese as is. But if you want to go one step further, set your broiler to low and transfer the cheesy macaroni to a 7 by 11-inch (18 by 28 cm) baking dish.

6. Put the almonds, coconut oil, and agave nectar in a food processor and process until the mixture has a mealy consistency. Scatter the mixture on top of the macaroni. Broil the mac and cheese for about 2 minutes, until the top is golden brown.

7. Garnish with fresh parsley and serve immediately. Leftovers can be kept in an airtight container in the fridge for up to 1 week.

THE BEST CAULIFLOWER MASH

IT MIGHT BE tough to imagine that anything could taste better than mashed potatoes. But cauliflower mash captures all the flavors of beloved potatoes, and you won't be able to taste the difference. Not only is this mash cheesy, buttery, and silky smooth, it also brings along a stellar lineup of vitamins and nutrients. Plus it's lower in carbohydrates and calories than its potato counterpart.

SERVES 4 TO 6

- 6 cups (810 g) cauliflower florets (see page 16)
- 8 garlic cloves
- 1 cup (120 g) shredded Cheddar
- ¼ cup (60 mL) heavy cream
- 2 tablespoons salted butter, plus more for serving
- ¼ teaspoon sea salt, plus more to taste
- ⅛ teaspoon freshly ground black pepper, plus more to taste
- 1 tablespoon chopped fresh chives, for garnish

1. Bring an inch of water to a boil in a large saucepan. Place the cauliflower in a steamer basket set over the boiling water. Cover and steam for about 5 minutes, until the florets are tender. Transfer the florets to a high-powered blender or food processor.

2. Add the garlic, cheese, heavy cream, butter, salt, and pepper to the cauliflower. Blend until smooth and creamy, 1 to 2 minutes. After 1 minute, if there are still chunks, use a rubber spatula to scrape down the sides, then process again until light, fluffy, and completely smooth. Taste and adjust the seasoning if needed.

3. Let the mash sit for 2 minutes to settle. Top with chives and serve with extra butter.

4. Leftovers can be kept in an airtight container in the refrigerator for up to 1 week.

GRILLED CAULIFLOWER KABOBS
WITH PEANUT SAUCE

PEANUT BUTTER MAKES everything taste better—even savory things. With the char from the grill and the tangy, sweet, nutty sauce, the cauliflower florets absorb all the peanut flavor. You'll need skewers for this recipe. The metal ones are easy to use and clean, but wooden skewers work as well; just remember to soak them for 30 minutes before grilling so they don't cook along with the food. Serve the kabobs alongside a main dish of chicken, steak, or fish.

SERVES 6

- 4 cups (540 g) medium cauliflower florets (see page 16)
- 2 tablespoons avocado oil
- 1 teaspoon garlic powder
- ½ cup (128 g) natural peanut butter
- Juice of ½ lime
- 2 tablespoons soy sauce or tamari
- 2 tablespoons unsweetened coconut cream
- 1 tablespoon agave nectar, honey, or maple syrup (see Note, page 25)
- ¼ teaspoon ground ginger
- ¼ teaspoon fish sauce
- Fresh cilantro leaves, for garnish
- Chopped peanuts, for garnish

1. Prepare a charcoal grill with hot coals or heat a gas grill on high for 5 to 10 minutes. Alternatively, heat a grill pan on the stovetop over high heat. If using wooden skewers, soak the skewers in water for at least 30 minutes.

2. Place the cauliflower florets in a large bowl and toss with the avocado oil and garlic powder to fully coat. Thread 4 to 6 florets on each of 6 skewers.

3. Lay a grill mat or piece of aluminum foil on the grill and place the kabobs on top. Grill for 5 minutes, then turn the kabobs and grill for another 5 minutes. The cauliflower should have dark brown marks in various places and be easily pierced with a fork. Transfer to a platter.

4. In a small bowl, whisk together the peanut butter, lime juice, soy sauce, coconut cream, agave nectar, ginger, and fish sauce. Drizzle the kabobs with the peanut sauce so they're well coated; transfer the remaining peanut sauce to a bowl for serving.

5. Sprinkle the kabobs with cilantro and chopped peanuts. Serve with the extra peanut sauce on the side.

CHEESY CAULIFLOWER AND GREEN BEAN CASSEROLE

CAULIFLOWER AND GREEN bean casserole is a dish that's easy enough to whip up for a weeknight side but delicious enough to serve for a holiday dinner. It's simple and flavorful and always a crowd pleaser. The sweet pecan crumble on top adds a crunchy contrast and also gives the casserole a homestyle feel.

SERVES 4 TO 6

- 3 tablespoons salted butter
- 6 cups (810 g) cauliflower florets (see page 16)
- 1 sweet onion, diced
- 1 cup (126 g) green beans, cut into 2-inch (5 cm) pieces
- ¼ cup (60 mL) chicken broth
- 2 garlic cloves, minced
- 1 cup (240 mL) heavy cream
- 1 cup (120 g) shredded Gruyère
- ¼ cup (30 g) shredded Parmesan
- ¼ teaspoon sea salt
- ⅛ teaspoon freshly ground black pepper
- 1 cup (110 g) raw pecans
- 2 tablespoons agave nectar, coconut nectar, honey, or maple syrup (see Note, page 25)

1. Melt the butter in a large ovenproof skillet over medium-high heat. Add the cauliflower and cook for 5 minutes, stirring frequently. Add the onion and continue to cook for another 5 to 7 minutes, stirring frequently, until the onion is caramelized and the florets are browned.

2. Add the green beans, chicken broth, and garlic to the skillet. Cook for another 3 to 5 minutes, stirring occasionally, until all the broth is absorbed.

3. Add the cream, both cheeses (reserving about ¼ cup/ 30 g of Gruyère to sprinkle on top), and the salt and pepper to the skillet. Lower the heat to medium and continue to cook for about 5 minutes, stirring occasionally, until the sauce thickens. Meanwhile, heat the broiler on high.

4. While the sauce is thickening, place the pecans in a small skillet over medium heat. Toast for 3 to 5 minutes, stirring frequently, until the pecans are fragrant and smell nutty. Place the pecans and agave nectar in a food processor and process until chunky, about 20 seconds.

5. Once the cream sauce has thickened, pour it over the veggies in the skillet. Sprinkle the reserved Gruyère over the top along with the toasted pecans. Broil for 2 minutes, until the top is bubbling and browned.

6. Leftovers can be stored in an airtight container in the fridge for about a week. Reheat in a microwave or sauté in a pan over medium-high heat, stirring frequently for about 3 minutes.

CAULIFLOWER CAPRESE
WITH PISTACHIO PESTO

· ·

CAPRESE IS THE perfect summer salad of tomato, mozzarella, and basil. This version is eaten warm and gets an interesting twist from both cauliflower and the pistachio pesto. It's a beautiful play of textures, flavors, and colors.

SERVES 4 TO 6

- 2 tablespoons avocado oil
- 5 cups (675 g) cauliflower florets (see page 16)

FOR THE PISTACHIO PESTO

- 1 cup (152 g) roasted, salted pistachios
- 2 tablespoons agave nectar, coconut nectar, honey, or maple syrup (see Note, page 25)
- ¼ cup (60 mL) refined coconut oil

- 8 ounces (227 g) small mozzarella balls, packed in water or oil and drained (sliced or shredded mozzarella or mozzarella "pearls" work too)
- 1 cup (142 g) grape tomatoes, sliced in half crosswise
- Bread or pita chips, for serving (optional)

1. In a large skillet, heat the avocado oil over medium-high heat. Add the florets and cook, stirring occasionally, for 10 minutes, until browned. Add 2 tablespoons water and continue to cook, stirring until all the water has evaporated and the florets are tender, about 5 minutes. Reduce the heat to low.

2. Meanwhile, make the pesto. Put the pistachios, agave nectar, and coconut oil in a food processor and process for about 30 seconds, until combined but still chunky.

3. Add the pistachio pesto to the pan with the cauliflower and toss. Add the mozzarella and the tomatoes. Stir and continue to cook until the mozzarella just starts to get soft and stretchy, but still holds its mini ball shape. If using shredded or sliced mozzarella, heat just until the cheese is slightly melted. Serve, if you'd like, with crusty bread or pita chips on the side. Enjoy immediately while the cheese is warm.

GRILLED CAULIFLOWER STEAKS
WITH AVOCADO-CILANTRO SAUCE

CAULIFLOWER STEAKS ALLOW you to load on the sauce and toppings in a way that traditional florets can't. This avocado and cilantro sauce with cotija cheese is light and summery, but you could change the toppings with the seasons (see Variations). Serve these steaks alongside salmon or serve two cauliflower steaks per person for a vegetarian meal.

SERVES 4

FOR THE CAULIFLOWER STEAKS

- 4 cauliflower steaks (see page 15); cut in ½ inch slices, reserve any additional florets that fall from the head as you slice
- 3 tablespoons avocado oil
- Sea salt and freshly ground black pepper
- 1 ear of corn, shucked
- 1 teaspoon smoked paprika
- 2 tablespoons crumbled cotija cheese
- 1 tablespoon chopped fresh cilantro leaves, for garnish

FOR THE AVOCADO-CILANTRO SAUCE

- ¼ cup (60 mL) unsweetened coconut cream
- 1 avocado
- Juice of 1 lime

(continued)

1. Prepare a charcoal grill with hot coals or heat a gas grill on high while you prepare the steaks. Alternatively, heat a grill pan on the stovetop over high heat.

2. Bring a large pot of water to a boil. Blanch 2 of the cauliflower steaks for about 40 seconds, then transfer to a baking sheet. Repeat with the remaining cauliflower steaks and any extra florets that are left after cutting the steaks. Drizzle the blanched cauliflower with 2 tablespoons of the avocado oil, and season with salt and pepper to taste.

3. Season the ear of corn with the remaining 1 tablespoon avocado oil, salt, pepper, and paprika.

4. Set a grill mat or piece of aluminum foil on the grill and place the steaks, florets, and corn on top. Grill the steaks and florets for about 5 minutes per side, until the steaks are browned and charred. Transfer to the baking sheet. Flip the corn every 3 minutes. Once it has char spots and is a brighter yellow, about 9 minutes, remove from the grill and place on the baking sheet.

5. While the cauliflower and corn are grilling, make the sauce: The coconut cream should be smooth; if it's not, warm it in a microwave for about 30 seconds and

- ¼ cup (10 g) fresh cilantro leaves
- 2 garlic cloves
- ¼ teaspoon sea salt

stir it until it appears milky. Alternatively, you can warm it in a small pot over medium heat, whisking until smooth.

6. Place the coconut cream, avocado, lime juice, cilantro, garlic cloves, and salt in a food processor. Process for 10 seconds. Use a rubber spatula to scrape down the sides, then process for another 5 to 10 seconds, until combined and smooth. Set aside.

7. Once the corn has cooled, stand the ear upright on a cutting board and use a sharp knife to cut the kernels away from the cob.

8. Transfer the cauliflower steaks to plates. Place a dollop of the avocado-cilantro sauce on each steak. Top with the extra florets, corn kernels, crumbled cotija, and chopped cilantro.

VARIATIONS

In fall, top cauliflower steaks with pumpkin spice pecan topping (process 1 cup raw pecans, ⅓ cup refined coconut oil, 2 tablespoons agave nectar, ½ teaspoon pumpkin spice, and ¼ teaspoon sea salt in a food processor for about 30 seconds until combined and smooth), toasted pepitas, and dried cranberries.

In colder weather, try the steaks with melted Gruyère cheese, fried prosciutto, toasted hazelnuts, and chopped fresh sage.

For a spring side, top steaks with Sun-Dried Tomato Pesto (page 148), sliced avocado, toasted pine nuts, and Smoked Chickpea Croutons (page 84).

SAVORY CHURROS

WITH GARLIC-DIJON AÏOLI

....

SAVORY CHURROS ARE a unique spin on the classic sweet treat. Think of them as upgraded French fries and serve them alongside a burger with an aïoli dipping sauce. The inside of the churro stays doughy while the outside gets crispy. You can get those iconic churro ridges by using a piping bag fitted with a large star tip. If you don't have a piping bag, cut the corner off a large ziptop plastic bag.

MAKES 10 CHURROS
....

FOR THE CHURROS

- 2 cups (270 g) cauliflower florets (see page 16)

- 3 garlic cloves

- 1 shallot, finely chopped

- 1 large egg

- 1½ cups (172 g) blanched almond flour (see Note, page 31)

- ½ teaspoon cayenne

- ½ teaspoon sea salt, plus more to finish

- 2½ cups (600 mL) safflower oil or your favorite frying oil

- 2 coarsely chopped basil leaves, for garnish

FOR THE GARLIC-DIJON AÏOLI

- ¼ cup (54 g) mayonnaise

- 1 tablespoon lemon juice

- 1 tablespoon Dijon mustard

- 1 teaspoon minced garlic

- Sea salt and freshly ground black pepper

1. Bring an inch of water to a boil in a medium saucepan. Place the cauliflower and garlic cloves in a steamer basket set over the boiling water. Cover and steam for about 5 minutes, until the florets are easily pierced with a fork.

2. Transfer the florets and garlic to a food processor and process for about 20 seconds, until the cauliflower is completely chopped into meal (see page 19).

3. Transfer the meal to a clean, thin dish towel or piece of cheesecloth and set it in a strainer in the sink for about 5 minutes to cool.

4. Meanwhile, whisk together the shallot and egg in a medium bowl. Set aside.

5. Once the cauliflower meal is cool enough to handle, gather the corners of the dish towel and, working over the sink, squeeze to remove any excess liquid. Place the squeezed meal in the bowl with the shallot and egg. Use a rubber spatula to fold the ingredients together.

6. Add the almond flour, cayenne, and sea salt. Fold until combined.

CONTINUED ·····················

7. Transfer the batter to a large piping bag or a 1-gallon plastic storage bag. Use a ½-inch (1 cm) star tip opening or cut off the corner of the plastic bag so the opening is about ½ inch (1 cm) in diameter.

8. In a large skillet, heat the oil over high heat for 3 to 5 minutes, until it starts to bubble on the bottom.

9. Working in batches, squeeze three 4-inch (10 cm) churros into the oil, using a butter knife to slice off the batter from the piping bag and letting it drop completely into the oil.

10. Fry for 1 to 2 minutes, until the bottom is golden brown. Flip the churros and cook the other side for another minute. Use a wire mesh skimmer to remove the churros from the oil and place on a paper towel–lined plate. Immediately sprinkle with sea salt. Repeat with the remaining batter.

11. Make the aïoli: In a small bowl, whisk together the mayonnaise, lemon juice, Dijon mustard, garlic, and salt and pepper to taste. Serve the dip with the hot churros. Garnish the churros with chopped basil.

12. Churros will keep in an airtight container in the fridge for about a week. Reheat in a large skillet over medium-high heat with 1 tablespoon of butter or oil. Stir occasionally for about 3 to 5 minutes, until heated through and the outside regains some crispness. Any leftover aïoli should be stored separately.

FRIED FLORETS

WITH GREEN GODDESS DRESSING

CAULIFLOWER CAN BE the queen of reinvention. If you think a floret is just a floret, fry some up and pair them with a creamy green goddess dressing.

SERVES 6

- 1½ cups (360 mL) avocado oil
- 2 tablespoons salted butter
- 6 cups (810 g) medium cauliflower florets (see page 16)

FOR THE GREEN GODDESS DRESSING

- 1 avocado
- ¼ cup (61 g) whole-milk yogurt
- 2 garlic cloves
- Juice of 1 lime
- ½ cup (20 g) fresh cilantro leaves, plus more for serving
- Sea salt and freshly ground black pepper

1. In a large frying pan, combine the oil and butter over high heat. Once the oil shimmers, reduce the heat to medium-high.

2. Place half of the florets in the oil in a single layer. Fry for about 5 minutes, until they turn golden brown. Use tongs to flip the florets to fry the other side. Cook for another 2 to 3 minutes. When both sides are golden brown, transfer the florets to a paper towel–lined plate and fry the second batch.

3. While the florets are frying, make the dressing: Combine the avocado, yogurt, garlic, lime juice, cilantro, and salt and pepper to taste in a food processor. Process for about 15 seconds. Use a rubber spatula to scrape down the sides, then process for another 15 seconds until the sauce is creamy but still shows flecks of cilantro.

4. Transfer the fried florets to a serving dish. Serve the green goddess dressing alongside or dolloped on top of the cauliflower. Garnish with some extra cilantro.

GARLIC NAAN

NAAN IS A traditionally leavened, oven-baked flatbread that is often served with Indian and other Central and South Asian foods. This version of garlic naan is made with cauliflower to provide the nutritious base, along with almond and arrowroot flours. Incorporating arrowroot flour gives the naan an airy lightness and a pull-apart texture reminiscent of traditional naan. Serve naan alongside curry or chili and use it to dip, dunk, or drag along your plate to soak up any extra sauce.

MAKES 4 NAAN

- 2 cups (270 g) cauliflower florets (see page 16)
- 1 large egg
- 10 garlic cloves, minced
- 2 cups (230 g) blanched almond flour (see Note, page 31)
- 1 cup (123 g) arrowroot flour (see Note, page 93)
- 2 teaspoons sea salt
- 2 tablespoons extra-virgin olive oil

1. Preheat the oven to 350°F (180°C) and line a baking sheet with parchment paper.

2. Bring a small pot of water to a boil. Add the florets to the pot and boil for about 5 minutes, until tender. Drain well.

3. Transfer the florets to a food processor and process until all the florets are completely chopped into a fine meal (see page 19). Use a rubber spatula to scrape down the sides of the food processor. Add the egg and 6 of the garlic cloves. Process again for another 30 seconds.

4. Add the almond flour, arrowroot flour, and 1 teaspoon of the salt. Process again until the ingredients combine and a dough forms, about 30 seconds. Transfer the dough to a bowl.

5. Use a spatula to roughly divide the dough into fourths. One quarter at a time, place the dough on the lined baking sheet and use damp hands to form it into a round, about 1/4 inch (6 mm) thick and 5 to 6 inches (12 to 15 cm) in diameter.

6. Working in batches of two on each baking sheet, bake for 15 to 20 minutes, until the edges appear golden brown.

7. Remove the naan from the oven and allow it to sit on the baking sheet for 5 minutes before drizzling with extra-virgin olive oil and sprinkling with a quarter of the remaining garlic and ¼ teaspoon salt. Repeat with the remaining dough.

8. Naan is best eaten fresh, but can be kept in the refrigerator in an airtight container for up to 1 week or frozen for up to 3 months.

CHEDDAR-JALAPEÑO CAULIFLOWER BISCUITS

WHEN YOU ADD cauliflower to biscuit batter, you are not going to get a traditional, flaky biscuit. But you will get a no-fuss, chewy, cheesy biscuit that stands out in the breadbasket. The cauliflower keeps the batter moist as it cooks and the Cheddar makes this biscuit reminiscent of Brazilian cheese bread. Don't be surprised if you eat more of these biscuits than you do of the main course.

MAKES 18 BISCUITS

- 2½ cups (340 g) cauliflower florets (see page 16)
- 2 garlic cloves
- 8 tablespoons (1 stick/113 g) unsalted butter, cut into chunks (ghee or coconut oil also works)
- 2 large eggs
- 2 cups (226 g) arrowroot flour (see Note, page 93)
- 1 cup (115 g) blanched almond flour (see Note, page 31)
- ½ teaspoon baking soda
- ½ teaspoon sea salt
- 2 cups (240 g) shredded Cheddar
- 2 medium jalapeños, stemmed, seeded, and chopped

1. Preheat the oven to 350°F (180°C). Grease muffin tins with butter or line them with paper liners.

2. Bring an inch of water to a boil in a medium saucepan. Place the cauliflower and garlic in a steamer basket set over the boiling water. Cover and steam for 5 minutes, until the florets are tender. Put the florets, garlic, and butter in a high-powered blender. Blend until smooth. Add the eggs and blend again until combined.

3. Add the arrowroot flour, almond flour, baking soda, and salt. Blend again until smooth. Fold in 1½ cups (180 g) of the Cheddar, reserving some for the tops of the biscuits. Fold in the chopped jalapeño.

4. Fill the muffin tins three-quarters full with batter. Sprinkle the reserved cheese on top. Bake for about 25 minutes, until the tops puff up and the muffins are cooked through. Transfer to a rack to cool for 5 minutes before serving.

5. Leftovers can be kept in an airtight container in the fridge for up to 1 week or frozen for up to 3 months.

6

DESSERTS

UNEXPECTED, I KNOW. To some, the concept of cauliflower playing a key role in dessert recipes borders on an oxymoron. But if avocados, sweet potatoes, black beans, and chickpeas can transform traditional treats into nutritious, indulgent desserts, why not cauliflower? Cauliflower acts as a substitute for oil or dairy in baked recipes. In other desserts, like the rice pudding or cookies, the cauliflower adds an essential texture to the treat. Try some and be convinced!

.... ✳ ....

CANDIED CAULIFLOWER BITES

THESE CAULI BITES are a sweet treat you can feel good about eating. Cauliflower florets are slow-roasted to crisp up in the oven and then tossed with a sweet cinnamon sauce that makes them an addictingly sweet snack. Eat them on their own or scatter the bites over your favorite ice cream or pudding for a sweet and nutritious topping.

MAKES 1 CUP

- 3 cups (405 g) small cauliflower florets (see page 16)
- 3 tablespoons refined coconut oil
- 1 teaspoon ground cinnamon
- ½ teaspoon sea salt
- 1 tablespoon coconut sugar
- 1 tablespoon agave nectar, honey, or maple syrup (see Note, page 25)

1. Preheat the oven to 300°F (150°C). Line a baking sheet with parchment paper.

2. In a medium bowl, toss the florets with 2 tablespoons of the coconut oil, cinnamon, and salt. Place in a single layer on the prepared baking sheet. Bake for 1 hour and 30 minutes, tossing the florets every 30 minutes. The florets will dry out a bit and get crispy on the outside.

3. Turn off the oven, leave the oven door ajar, and allow the florets to come to room temperature in the oven.

4. In a small bowl, whisk together the remaining tablespoon of coconut oil, the coconut sugar, and agave nectar. Drizzle the mixture over the florets and toss until they're evenly coated.

5. Store the bites in an airtight container in the fridge for up to 2 weeks. The coconut oil will solidify in the cold. Warm them up in the microwave or in the oven at a low temperature to remelt the sauce before eating any leftovers.

VANILLA CARAMEL PUDDING

IF YOU WANT a make-ahead dessert for the holidays or to serve at any party, you'll love the flavor and indulgence of this vanilla caramel pudding. This version has all the decadent flavors of a traditional flan, but the consistency has a bit more texture. Bake the pudding in ramekins or little dishes so each person gets an individual dessert.

SERVES 4

- 2 cups (270 g) cauliflower florets (see page 16)
- 1 pint (480 mL) heavy cream
- ½ cup (80 g) coconut sugar
- 5 large egg yolks
- ½ teaspoon vanilla bean powder
- ½ teaspoon sea salt
- 1 cup Homemade Whipped Cream (page 44)

1. Preheat the oven to 350°F (180°C).

2. Bring an inch of water to a boil in a medium saucepan. Place the cauliflower in a steamer basket set over the boiling water. Cover and steam for about 5 minutes, until the florets are easily pierced with a fork.

3. Place the florets in a high-powered blender. Add the heavy cream and coconut sugar and blend until smooth, about 10 seconds. Add the egg yolks, vanilla bean powder, and sea salt and blend again until smooth, about 15 seconds.

4. Place 4 ramekins on a baking sheet. Pour the batter into the ramekins until they're three-quarters full. Bake for about 40 minutes, until the tops are set and browned. They'll still be a bit jiggly, but the tops should not look wet.

5. Allow the pudding to sit out and come to room temperature for 30 minutes to 1 hour. Then cover the ramekins with foil and refrigerate for at least 3 hours and up to 2 days before serving.

6. Serve with a dollop of whipped cream.

CHOCOLATE MOUSSE

CAULIFLOWER MAKES THIS mousse extra creamy. And if you want a dairy-free choc-olate mousse, you can substitute chilled coconut cream for the heavy cream. Plan ahead and and prep this recipe the night before you want to serve it. The mousse needs to set overnight so that it whips into the proper consistency.

SERVES 8

- 2 cups (270 g) cauliflower florets (see page 16)

- 1 pint (480 mL) heavy cream, or 1 13.5-ounce (398 mL) can unsweetened coconut cream, chilled

- 1½ cups (255 g) 60% cacao dark chocolate chips

- ¼ cup (60 mL) refined coconut oil

- 3 tablespoons agave nectar, honey, or maple syrup (see Note, page 25)

- 1 tablespoon tapioca flour

- 1 teaspoon vanilla extract

- A couple of pinches fine sea salt

- ¼ cup (44 g) shaved 60% cacao dark chocolate, for topping

- Flaked sea salt, for topping

1. Bring an inch of water to a boil in a medium saucepan. Place the cauliflower in a steamer basket set over the boiling water. Cover and steam for 5 minutes, until the florets are easily pierced with a fork.

2. Place the steamed florets, cream, chocolate chips, coconut oil, agave nectar, tapioca flour, vanilla, and salt in a high-powered blender. Blend for about 1 minute, until the mixture is completely smooth and creamy.

3. Transfer the mousse to a covered dish and chill for at least 3 hours or overnight.

4. Before serving, scoop the mousse into the bowl of a stand mixer fitted with the paddle attachment (or into a large bowl, if using a handheld mixer) and whip it on high for 2 minutes. The mousse should be light and fluffy.

5. Transfer the mixture to a piping bag with a large tip or a plastic bag with one corner cut off and pipe it in a circular, swirling motion into small serving dishes. Top with dark shaved chocolate and flaked sea salt.

6. Leftovers can be kept in an airtight container in the fridge for up to 1 week.

SALTED CARAMEL FONDUE

WITH FRUIT SKEWERS

....

FONDUE IS A versatile dessert because it's delicious not only as a warm dip, but in countless other ways as well. As a dip you can pair it with anything from fruit to chocolate—even pound cake. Or you can drizzle it on top of a bowl of ice cream or your favorite brownies or cookies. Any fine skewers you have on hand—wooden, metal, or even toothpicks—work for this recipe.

MAKES ABOUT 2½ CUPS FONDUE AND 8 SKEWERS; SERVES 4

- 2 cups (270 g) cauliflower florets (see page 16)
- 1 13.5-ounce (398 mL) can unsweetened coconut cream
- 1 cup (174 g) white chocolate chips
- ¼ cup (40 g) coconut sugar
- ½ teaspoon vanilla bean powder
- ½ teaspoon fine sea salt
- 1 cup (114 g) strawberries, hulled
- ½ cup (73 g) blueberries
- 1 cup (146 g) raspberries
- ½ cup (73 g) blackberries

1. Bring an inch of water to a boil in a medium saucepan. Place the cauliflower in a steamer basket set over the boiling water. Cover and steam the florets for 5 minutes, until they're easily pierced with a fork.

2. Transfer the steamed florets to a high-powered blender along with the coconut cream, white chocolate chips, coconut sugar, vanilla bean powder, and sea salt. Blend on high speed until smooth. Pour the mixture into a bowl and allow to sit out on the counter or place in the fridge to cool for about 20 minutes, so the mixture thickens.

3. Assemble the skewers with rows of alternating fruits. Serve the skewers with a bowl of fondue alongside. Once skewered, the fruit will keep for about 3 hours before breaking down, and any extra fondue can be stored in an airtight container in the refrigerator for up to 5 days.

TROPICAL KALE AND CAULIFLOWER POPSICLES

ONE OF MY first parenting wins when my kids were toddlers was sneaking vegetables into popsicles (cue evil winning laugh here). I'd blend up kale and tropical fruits, throw them into a popsicle mold, and brand them as dinosaur pops. Seeing my picky eaters consume those green popsicles and ask for more gave me a parenting high that, let's face it, can be hard to come by. This version adds cauliflower into the mix, which means even more veggies!

MAKES 12 POPSICLES

- 3 cups (405 g) cauliflower florets (see page 16)
- 1⅓ cups (320 mL) unsweetened coconut cream
- 2 large leaves curly kale, stemmed
- 1 banana, frozen
- 1 cup (165 g) frozen pineapple
- 1 cup (165 g) frozen mango
- 1 tablespoon agave nectar, honey, or maple syrup (optional; see Note, page 25)

1. Bring an inch of water to a boil in a medium saucepan. Place the cauliflower in a steamer basket set over the boiling water. Cover and steam the florets for 5 minutes, until they're easily pierced with a fork.

2. Transfer the steamed cauliflower to a high-powered blender along with the coconut cream, kale, banana, pineapple, mango, and agave nectar, if using. Blend for 1 to 2 minutes, until completely smooth and creamy.

3. Pour into popsicle molds, add the sticks, and freeze overnight. They'll keep for about 1 month in the freezer.

STRAWBERRY ICE CREAM

STRAWBERRY (AND CAULIFLOWER!) ice cream can be served two ways. Eat it immediately straight from the blender for a creamy soft-serve, with an almost milkshake-like consistency. Or, transfer the mixture to a loaf pan and freeze it overnight to get that hard, scoopable ice cream texture.

MAKES 6 CUPS

- 2 cups (270 g) cauliflower florets (see page 16)
- 3 cups (340 g) frozen strawberries
- 1 pint (480 mL) heavy cream
- ¼ cup (83 g) agave nectar (see Note, page 25)
- ½ teaspoon vanilla bean powder
- ¼ teaspoon sea salt

1. Bring an inch of water to a boil in a medium saucepan. Place the cauliflower in a steamer basket set over the boiling water. Cover and steam the florets for about 5 minutes, until they're easily pierced with a fork.

2. Place the steamed cauliflower, strawberries, cream, agave nectar, vanilla bean powder, and salt in a high-powered blender and blend on high for 2 minutes, until the ingredients are creamy and smooth.

3. Eat immediately or transfer the mixture to a loaf pan covered tightly with plastic wrap and freeze overnight. When ready to serve, let the pan sit out on the counter for 5 to 10 minutes to soften before scooping it into cups or cones.

CAULIFLOWER RICE PUDDING

....

THIS ISN'T YOUR grandma's rice pudding . . . although I'm sure hers is delicious too. This modern rice pudding is loaded with superfoods—like chia seeds and hemp hearts—and packs a nutritious punch. Not only do the chia seeds add lots of fiber and other health benefits, but when they're soaked, they also give a gelatinous texture to the pudding. Play around with adding 2 tablespoons of cocoa powder or natural peanut butter to the pudding to change the flavor.

SERVES 4

- 1½ cups (360 mL) whole milk, full-fat coconut milk, or any nut milk

- 1 cup (105 g) cauliflower rice (see page 18)

- ¼ cup (83 g) agave nectar, honey, or maple syrup (see Note, page 25)

- ¼ cup (48 g) white chia seeds

- ¼ cup (40 g) hemp hearts

- ¼ cup (30 g) chopped hazelnuts (or any nut)

- ¼ cup (40 g) golden raisins (optional)

- ½ teaspoon ground cinnamon

- ½ teaspoon vanilla extract

- ¼ teaspoon ground ginger

- ¼ teaspoon sea salt

1. In a medium saucepan over high heat, combine the milk, cauliflower rice, and agave nectar. Bring to a boil, then reduce the heat to medium-low and let the mixture simmer for about 5 minutes, stirring occasionally, until the cauliflower is cooked through.

2. Add the chia seeds, hemp hearts, hazelnuts, raisins, cinnamon, vanilla, ginger, and salt to the pot. Stir for another 3 minutes, until well combined. If the pudding begins to thicken up too much, add more milk to thin it.

3. Serve warm, spooned into individual bowls. Cover and store any leftovers in the fridge for up to 5 days.

CHOCOLATE PEANUT BUTTER CHEESECAKE SQUARES

CHEESECAKE SQUARES ARE the perfect make-ahead dessert. I usually cut these into sixteen servings for smaller bite-size pieces, but for a larger, more decadent dessert, consider cutting them into 9 larger squares. Make the cheesecake the night before you want to serve these so they have enough time to chill.

MAKES SIXTEEN 2¼-INCH SQUARES

FOR THE CRUST

- 2 cups (270 g) cauliflower rice (see page 18)
- 2 tablespoons salted butter
- 1 cup (115 g) blanched almond flour (see Note, page 31)
- ½ cup (57 g) finely chopped hazelnuts
- ½ cup (57 g) finely chopped pecans
- ¼ cup (24 g) cocoa powder
- ¼ cup (40 g) coconut sugar
- ¼ cup (83 g) agave nectar (see Note, page 25)
- ½ teaspoon ground cinnamon
- ½ teaspoon sea salt

FOR THE FILLING

- 24 ounces (680 g) cream cheese, at room temperature
- ¼ cup (83 g) agave nectar
- ¼ cup (40 g) coconut sugar

(continued)

1. Preheat the oven to 300°F (150°C). Line a 9 by 9-inch (23 by 23 cm) square pan with parchment paper, leaving an overhang on two sides for easy removal.

2. Make the crust: In a medium skillet over medium-high heat, combine the cauliflower rice and the butter. Cook for about 7 minutes, stirring frequently, until the rice turns translucent and has softened.

3. Transfer the cauliflower rice to a medium bowl and add the almond flour, hazelnuts, pecans, cocoa, coconut sugar, agave nectar, cinnamon, and salt. Fold the ingredients together until well combined.

4. Firmly press the mixture into the bottom of the prepared pan. Bake for 10 minutes, then set on a wire rack to cool.

5. Make the filling: In the bowl of a stand mixer fitted with the paddle attachment (or in a large bowl using a handheld electric mixer), cream the cream cheese, agave nectar, coconut sugar, peanut butter, and vanilla for about 1 minute. Add the eggs and use a handheld whisk to mix until smooth. (Switching to a handheld whisk to incorporate the eggs will ensure there will be fewer air bubbles and cracks in the top of the cheesecake.)

CONTINUED

- ¼ cup (64 g) natural peanut butter

- 2 teaspoons vanilla extract

- 3 large eggs

FOR THE TOPPING

- ¼ cup (64 g) natural peanut butter

- 2 teaspoons refined coconut oil

- ¼ cup (44 g) dark chocolate chips

6. Pour the cream cheese mixture on top of the baked crust and use a spatula to spread it evenly to the edges. Bake for 40 minutes. Allow the cheesecake to cool at room temperature for 40 minutes, then chill in the fridge for about 1 hour.

7. Meanwhile, make the topping: In a small bowl, combine the peanut butter and 1 teaspoon of coconut oil. In a second small bowl, place the dark chocolate chips and remaining 1 teaspoon of coconut oil. Warm each bowl for 1 to 2 minutes in the microwave or in a double boiler, stirring every 30 seconds, until the contents are melted.

8. Drizzle the peanut butter and chocolate back and forth across the top of the cheesecake.

9. When you're ready to serve, slide a knife around the two edges without the parchment overhang and pull the ends of the parchment paper up to remove the cheesecake from the pan. Cut into 16 squares.

10. The cheesecake will keep in an airtight container in the fridge for up to 1 week.

CAULIFLOWER DESSERT PIZZA

WE ALL KNOW a cauliflower crust can be a perfect stand-in for a traditional pizza crust, but it makes a darn good dessert pizza base too. Try this crust with different toppings, like sliced bananas and peanut butter or your favorite jam, sprinkled with some chopped pecans. Load it up with chocolate chips, nuts, and fruit and enjoy a slice just like you would your favorite pizza.

SERVES 6

FOR THE CRUST

- 4 cups (540 g) cauliflower florets (see page 16)
- 3 large eggs
- 1 cup (120 g) shredded Gruyère
- 1 cup (115 g) blanched almond flour (see Note, page 31)
- 3 tablespoons coconut sugar
- ½ teaspoon ground cinnamon
- ¼ teaspoon sea salt
- 2 tablespoons refined coconut oil, melted

FOR THE TOPPINGS

- 1 cup (174 g) 60% cacao dark chocolate chips, melted
- 5 strawberries, cut horizontally into rounds
- ¼ cup (37 g) blueberries
- ¼ cup (37 g) blackberries
- ¼ cup (36 g) toasted hazelnuts, chopped

1. Preheat the oven to 450°F (230°C). Line a baking sheet with parchment paper.

2. Working in batches, process the florets in a food processor until they are completely chopped into meal (see page 19). Place the cauliflower meal in a loosely covered microwave-safe bowl. Microwave on high for 4 minutes. Allow to cool for a few minutes. Alternatively, you can steam the florets for 5 minutes until tender, let cool, then pulse in the food processor to make the meal.

3. Transfer the cooled cauliflower meal to a clean, thin dish towel or piece of cheesecloth and, working over the sink, squeeze out all the excess liquid.

4. In a large bowl, combine the squeezed cauliflower, eggs, cheese, almond flour, coconut sugar, cinnamon, and salt.

5. Transfer the mixture to the baking sheet. Using your hands, form the mixture into a pizza-shaped round. Pat and press around the edges to smooth them out. You want the crust to be about 12 inches (30 cm) in diameter and ¼ to ½ inch (6 to 12 mm) thick.

CONTINUED

6. Brush the edges of the crust with the melted coconut oil and bake for 15 minutes. If the center is not already browned from baking, broil on high for 2 minutes.

7. Remove the crust from the oven and top with the melted chocolate, berries, and nuts. Once toppings are added, dessert pizza is best enjoyed immediately. Well wrapped, the crust (without any toppings) will keep in the fridge for about 1 week.

1. Pour the melted chocolate on top of the baked cauliflower crust.

2. Use the back of a spoon to smooth the chocolate into an even layer across the crust.

3. Top with sliced strawberries, blueberries, blackberries, raspberries, or any fruit that is in season.

4. Sprinkle with chopped hazelnuts and cut into slices to enjoy.

PEANUT BUTTER MUFFINS

THESE MUFFINS ARE moist and fluffy but with a concentrated peanut butter flavor that reminds me of the most decadent peanut butter cookies. The fact that they are made completely in a blender makes them super easy to whip up and clean up. Although these muffins taste like an indulgent dessert, the batter is packed with wholesome ingredients, including protein and fiber, so you could eat them for breakfast the next morning too.

MAKES 12 MUFFINS

- 2 cups (270 g) cauliflower florets (see page 16)
- 1 cup (256 g) natural peanut butter
- ½ cup (80 g) coconut sugar
- ⅓ cup (98 g) coconut nectar (see Note, page 25)
- 1 large egg
- ½ teaspoon vanilla extract
- ½ cup (57 g) blanched almond flour (see Note, page 31)
- ½ teaspoon baking soda
- 1 cup (117 g) chopped walnuts
- ¾ cup (134 g) peanut butter chips

1. Preheat the oven to 350°F (180°C). Spray a 12-cup muffin tin with cooking spray or line the cups with muffin liners.

2. Bring an inch of water to a boil in a medium saucepan. Place the cauliflower in a steamer basket set over the boiling water. Cover and steam the florets for about 5 minutes, until they're easily pierced with a fork.

3. While the florets are steaming, place the peanut butter, coconut sugar, coconut nectar, egg, and vanilla in a high-powered blender. Blend for about 20 seconds, until combined.

4. Add the steamed florets to the blender and blend on high for another 30 seconds, until the batter is smooth and combined.

5. Add the almond flour and baking soda to the blender. Blend again for about 10 seconds to incorporate the dry ingredients. If needed, use a rubber spatula to scrape down the sides, then blend for 10 additional seconds until fully combined.

6. Use a long-handled spatula to fold in the walnuts and ½ cup (84 g) of the peanut butter chips.

7. Scoop the batter into the prepared muffin cups until they're about three-quarters full. Top each muffin with the remaining peanut butter chips.

8. Bake for 20 minutes, until the tops appear set; the muffin tops should bounce back when you touch them. Transfer to a cooling rack.

9. The muffins can be stored in an airtight container in the fridge for about 1 week.

CHUNKY CHAI WHITE CHOCOLATE COOKIES

COOKIES THAT ARE loaded with crunchy nuts and chocolate are some of my favorites. Here, dehydrated cauliflower rice is blended with shredded coconut, chopped pecans, and white chocolate chips to create a sweet and textured cookie.

MAKES 12 COOKIES

- 3 cups (315 g) cauliflower rice (see page 18)
- 8 tablespoons (1 stick/113 g) unsalted butter, at room temperature
- ½ cup (80 g) coconut sugar
- 2 large eggs
- 1 teaspoon vanilla extract
- 1 cup (115 g) blanched almond flour (see Note, page 31)
- 3 teaspoons ground cinnamon
- 1 teaspoon ground ginger
- ¼ teaspoon ground cardamom
- ⅔ cup (56 g) unsweetened shredded coconut
- 1 cup (114 g) chopped pecans
- ½ cup (87 g) white chocolate chips

1. Preheat the oven to 300°F (150°C). Line a baking sheet with parchment paper.

2. Spread the cauliflower rice evenly across the prepared baking sheet and bake for 1 hour and 30 minutes, stirring every 20 minutes so that it toasts evenly. When the rice is dehydrated and lightly toasted, remove it from the oven and set aside for 15 minutes until it cools to room temperature.

3. Raise the oven temperature to 350°F (180°C). Line a second baking sheet with parchment paper.

4. Place the toasted rice in a food processor and process for 30 seconds to make the pieces a bit smaller and more uniform.

5. Transfer the rice to a large bowl and add the butter, coconut sugar, eggs, and vanilla. Whisk until combined.

6. Add the almond flour, cinnamon, ginger, and cardamom. Whisk again until combined. Fold in the coconut, pecans, and white chocolate chips, reserving some of the chips and pecans for the tops of the cookies.

7. Use a small ice cream scoop or a tablespoon to scoop 6 cookies onto the prepared baking sheet. Use your fingers to gently press the tops down. Sprinkle with

the reserved chips and pecans. Bake for about 12 minutes, until the edges are golden brown and the centers are dry.

8. Allow the cookies to cool on the baking sheet for 5 minutes before transferring them to a cooling rack. Repeat with the rest of the cookie dough.

9. The cookies can be stored in an airtight container in the fridge for up to 1 week.

DOUBLE-CHOCOLATE BROWNIES

USING CAULIFLOWER AS a base makes for brownies that are not only supercreamy, moist, and rich-tasting but also dairy- and oil-free. Serve them with a scoop of ice cream and a drizzle of homemade Caramel Sauce (page 35) to make a brownie sundae.

MAKES NINE 3-INCH BROWNIES

- 3 cups (405 g) cauliflower florets (see page 16)
- 3 large eggs
- ½ cup (80 g) coconut sugar
- ¼ cup (83 g) agave nectar, honey, or maple syrup (see Note, page 25)
- 1 cup (115 g) blanched almond flour (see Note, page 31)
- ½ cup (48 g) cocoa powder
- 1 teaspoon baking soda
- ½ teaspoon sea salt
- ¾ cup (131 g) 60% cacao dark chocolate chips

1. Preheat the oven to 350°F (180°C). Line a 9 by 9-inch (23 by 23 cm) square pan with parchment paper, leaving an overhang on two sides for easy removal.

2. Bring an inch of water to a boil in a medium saucepan. Place the cauliflower in a steamer basket set over the boiling water. Cover and steam the florets for about 5 minutes, until they're easily pierced with a fork. Remove the steamer basket and set aside for 10 minutes to cool.

3. Place the eggs, coconut sugar, and agave nectar in a blender. Blend on high for about 10 seconds, until combined. Add the steamed florets and blend again until smooth.

4. Add the almond flour, cocoa powder, baking soda, and salt to the blender. Blend again until the dry ingredients are completely incorporated. Use a long-handled spatula to fold in ½ cup (87 g) of the chocolate chips.

5. Pour the brownie batter into the prepared pan. Spread it evenly across the pan and into the corners. Sprinkle the remaining chocolate chips on top.

6. Bake for 30 minutes, until the edges start to pull away from the pan and the top springs back when lightly pressed. Remove from the oven and allow to sit in the pan for 5 minutes before pulling up both ends of the parchment paper and placing the brownies on a cooling rack. Let cool for another 5 minutes before cutting the brownies into 9 large squares.

7. The brownies can be stored in an airtight container in the fridge for up to 1 week.

RESOURCES

I LOVE THAT specialty food items are more accessible than ever before. I don't often have time to wander aimlessly through my grocery store searching for items, so I typically order my ingredients from online retailers. Here are some brands I buy and use regularly.

Agave nectar
Wholesome
wholesomesweet.com

Arrowroot flour/starch
Bob's Red Mill
www.bobsredmill.com

Avocado oil
Chosen Foods
chosenfoods.com

Blanched almond flour
Wellbee's
www.wellbees.com

Bob's Red Mill
www.bobsredmill.com

Cassava flour
Otto's Naturals
www.ottosnaturals.com

Chia seeds
Salba Chia
www.salbasmart.com

Chickpea pasta
Banza
www.eatbanza.com

Coconut nectar
Big Tree Farms
www.bigtreefarms.com

Coconut oil
Nutiva
www.nutiva.com

Coconut sugar
Anthony's Goods
www.anthonysgoods.com

Flax seeds
Bob's Red Mill
www.bobsredmill.com

Ghee
Fourth & Heart
fourthandheart.com

Hemp hearts
Manitoba Harvest
manitobaharvest.com

Liquid smoke
Colgin
www.colgin.com

Nutritional yeast
Bob's Red Mill
www.bobsredmill.com

Tamari
San-J
san-j.com

Tapioca flour/starch
Anthony's Goods
www.anthonysgoods.com

Unsweetened coconut cream
Native Forest
store.edwardandsons.com

Vanilla bean powder
Kiva
www.kivahealthfood.com

ACKNOWLEDGMENTS

To Jaryd, for always encouraging me to go big and pursue what I love fearlessly. Not in my wildest dreams did I think this would be our path, but every day I thank my lucky stars I get to do life with you.

To Caleb and Nolan, thank you for always giving me something to smile about. Thank you for snuggly mornings and nightly dance parties. Thank you for making me work extra hard to get your stamp of approval on these recipes. This cookbook is better because of your high standards.

To my mom, for teaching me that a good recipe is worth sharing. To my dad, for showing me that nothing good comes without hard work. To my brother, for sharing and encouraging my entrepreneurial spirit. Thank you.

To my friends and family who have supported The Toasted Pine Nut since day one, even when I had no clue what I was doing. Thank you.

I am eternally grateful to the incredibly charming, smart, perceptive, generous, creative, engaging, and kind readers of *The Toasted Pine Nut*. Thank you for allowing me to share my life, my recipes, and my love for gooey chocolate chip cookies with you. Without you, this book would have never happened.

To Leigh Eisenman, thank you for knowing I was the right person for this project, for being rightfully excited about cauliflower, and for your dedication to this book. Your friendship has guided me through this process, and I am incredibly grateful to you.

To Judy Pray, thank you for shaping my recipes and words into this beautiful book. I am a newbie to the cookbook world and your passion and expertise have been truly inspiring.

To Lauren Volo, thank you for taking gorgeous images that make the recipes appear as dreamy and exciting as they taste. I loved chasing light with you.

To Caroline Hwang, thank you for styling even the ugliest orange dish to look beautiful and for casually carrying a blowtorch in your bag. You saved the day on more than one occasion.

To Michelle Cohen and the entire Artisan publishing team, thank you for making this book an absolute stunner. It has been a joy to see it come alive in a way I never imagined. Thank you for believing in this project.

INDEX

LINDSAY GRIMES FREEDMAN is a former attorney turned full-time blogger and social media presence who discovered the power of cauliflower while exploring new ways to feed her family after her husband's diagnosis of type 1 diabetes. You can find her on Instagram and YouTube @thetoastedpinenut.